Management and Competition in the NHS

Second Edition

Chris Ham

*Professor of Health Policy and Management
and Director of the Health Services Management Centre,
University of Birmingham*

Radcliffe Medical Press

© 1997 Chris Ham

Radcliffe Medical Press Ltd
18 Marcham Road, Abingdon, Oxon OX14 1AA, UK

Radcliffe Medical Press, Inc.
141 Fifth Avenue, New York, NY 10010, USA

First edition 1994

British Library Cataloguing in Publication Data

A catalogue record for this book is available from the British Library.

ISBN 1 85775 104 3

Typeset by AMA Graphics Ltd, Preston
Printed and bound in Great Britain by
Biddles Ltd, Guildford and King's Lynn

To Matthew

Contents

List of Figures, Boxes and Table

Figures

Boxes

Table

Introduction to the first edition

The New National Health Service: organization and management was published in 1990 and provided a description of the reforms announced in *Working for Patients* and an introduction to the NHS (Ham, 1990a). This new book is a sequel and, in writing it, I have departed significantly from the original format. In part, this is because I have since collaborated in the production of a guide to the NHS (Ham and Haywood, 1992) which covers much of the same ground, and in part because it seemed more important at this stage to go beyond description and to seek to evaluate the reforms. The change of title reflects this different approach.

For the last six years I feel I have lived and breathed the NHS reforms. From Margaret Thatcher's decision to set up a review of the NHS in 1988, through publication of *Working for Patients* in 1989 and the anticipation of the reforms coming into operation in 1991, there can have been no more exciting time to be a health policy analyst. Add to that the experience of observing the 1991 reforms in action, and it has been an unprecedented period in the development of the NHS.

During those six years I have been involved in the process of reform in a variety of ways. Initially, at the King's Fund Institute, I worked with colleagues to analyse the options facing the government and to make an initial assessment of *Working for Patients* (Ham *et al.*, 1989). This included a major study of the performance of health services in Europe and North America (Ham, Robinson and Benzeval, 1990).

Leading on from this, I contributed to the implementation of the reforms through my work at the King's Fund College with civil servants, health service managers and health care professionals. This work focused in particular on the development of the role of district health authorities as purchasers and it resulted in a series of reports on experience as it emerged in different parts of the NHS. These activities have continued since my move to the Health Services Management Centre at the University of Birmingham in 1992. Through a combination of research, consultancy and seminars I have maintained a close interest in the evolution of the reforms at all levels. In the course of a typical working week, this means spending three or four days in the field, working with purchasers, providers and others, both learning about what is happening in the NHS and passing on the benefits of this experience to those charged with making the reforms work.

In view of the rapid pace of change, I decided at an early stage to write up my observations and reflections on what was happening on a regular basis. The result has been a series of articles, papers and reports commenting on the reforms and trying to make sense of their impact. This book draws together many of the ideas from these publications but it seeks to go beyond them in two ways: firstly, it attempts to assess the impact of the reforms as a whole, not simply individual elements within them; secondly, and more ambitiously, it draws on experience gained since 1991 to identify the lessons that emerge and to suggest what needs to be done to take the reforms forward.

In writing the book, I have drawn on the results of my own work and that of other academics. This is not, however, the product of a traditional research project. Rather, it is an attempt to pull together data and intelligence from a wide variety of sources, to paint a picture of the background and development of the reforms, and to make an initial assessment of their impact. This task has not been made easier by the limited amount of research evidence available (the government always refused to support evaluation of the reforms), nor by the evolutionary nature of the changes. In time, some of the judgements will need to be revised in the light of further experience and as new data become available. Nevertheless, at the time of writing they represent my best assessment of developments so far.

I have received valuable support from my colleagues at the Health Services Management Centre, Anne van der Salm and

Deirdra Keane, in the preparation of this manuscript. I am also grateful to Philip Hunt, Chris Robinson and Angela Sealey of NAHAT for their comments on a draft of the book. I would like to thank my family for allowing me to steal the time to do the writing. The book is dedicated to Matthew (age 4) who has been especially understanding. It is a family joke that his first words were 'white paper'.

Chris Ham
April 1994

Introduction to the second edition

In preparing the second edition I have concentrated on updating the text to take account of developments in the last three years. In so doing I have drawn on the results of published research as well as my own writings. As before, *Management and Competition in the NHS* seeks to provide a clear and brief introduction to the origins of the NHS reforms, their implementation and impact. The book also analyses the future of the reforms in the light of developments in both the Conservative and Labour parties towards the NHS. Chapter four has been completely rewritten to take account of these developments and to reflect the growing importance of primary care and the continuing debates about health care rationing. As an introduction to the reformed NHS, the book does not attempt to be comprehensive. Rather, it seeks to describe the way in which the main elements within the reforms have been implemented, and to summarize their effects. Readers seeking additional information can do so by following up the references and suggestions for further reading.

Once again, I would like to thank my colleagues at the Health Services Management Centre for their support in preparing the book, especially Anne van der Salm, Sarah Stewart and Kieran Walshe. I would also like to thank my family for their tolerance of my addiction to writing. Any faults and errors are of course my responsibility.

Chris Ham
March 1997

1 The Background to the NHS Reforms

The establishment of the NHS in 1948 was a bold attempt to make health services available to all citizens through a system of public finance and public provision. It was universal in its coverage and sought to be comprehensive in terms of the services that were available. To encourage the use of these services, there were no charges for treatment, at least initially, and it was the aim of the founders of the NHS to ensure that all necessary services were readily accessible in each area. The principle of equity was firmly enshrined in the structure of the NHS, meaning that care was to be provided on the basis of clinically defined need rather than ability to pay or other considerations. NHS finance was raised through a combination of taxes and insurance contributions, in the course of time supplemented by nominal charges for prescriptions, dental treatment and eye tests. A private health care sector continued to operate alongside the NHS but it remained a minor part of total health service finance and provision until the 1980s when it grew rapidly in response to the constraints imposed on the NHS.

The NHS in the 1980s

It was in the 1980s that the future of the NHS came under the critical scrutiny of Margaret Thatcher's governments. Administrative reorganizations in 1974 and 1982 sought to tackle weaknesses in the organization and management of health services whilst preserving the basic framework that had been put in place in 1948. Figure 1 illustrates the structure of the NHS in England as it emerged from the 1982 reorganization. In this structure, district health authorities were responsible for running hospital and community health services and family practitioner committees administered the contracts of GPs and other independent contractors. The performance of district health authorities and

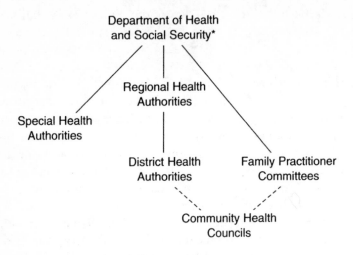

*The DHSS became the Department of Health in 1988

Figure 1: The structure of the NHS in England, 1982–90 (Source: Ham (1992a)).

family practitioner committees was supervised by regional health authorities and the Department of Health and Social Security. The result was a classic example of a centrally directed planning and management system involving hierarchical relationships between different levels of management and increasingly sophisticated efforts to get the organization right.

The first significant departure from this approach came with the *Griffiths Report* of 1983. This left the structure of the NHS unchanged and instead sought to respond to evidence of variations in efficiency and the lack of attention to quality through the introduction of general management. In essence, this was an attempt to make the NHS more businesslike (Roy Griffiths was Deputy Chairman and Managing Director of the Sainsbury's supermarket chain) through the adoption of management methods drawn from industry. The Griffiths reforms reflected a wider set of changes in the public sector during this period designed to control the growth of public expenditure, ensure that there was value for money in the use of public funds, and improve the quality of public services.

2

Throughout the 1980s expenditure on the NHS continued to grow in real terms but at a slow rate (*see* Table 1). As the decade wore on there was a widening gap between the money provided by government and the funding needed to meet increasing demands from an ageing population and advances in medical technology. The impact of the funding shortfall became particularly apparent during the course of 1987 and was felt most acutely in the hospital services (Ham, Robinson and Benzeval, 1990). In the autumn of that year, many health authorities had to take urgent action to keep expenditure within cash limits. This included cancelling non-emergency admissions, closing beds on a temporary basis, and not filling staff vacancies.

Behind these problems lay a funding system that failed to reward hospitals for treating extra patients. The so-called 'efficiency trap' was caused by the use of global budgets for hospitals that provided a fixed income regardless of the number of patients treated. This meant that hospitals were in practice penalized for productivity improvements because their expenditure increased in line with the number of patients treated but their income remained the same. In this situation, hospitals had little alternative but to reduce workload and cut costs when their budgets ran out.

The financial pressures facing health authorities were compounded by staff shortages. Media attention focused on Birmingham Children's Hospital where the shortage of specialist nurses meant that a number of children had their heart operations delayed. The parents of two of these children, David Barber and Matthew Collier, resorted to legal action in an attempt to bring the operations forward, but to no avail. Doctors added their voices to patients, demanding that something should be done. The British Medical Association called for additional resources to avert the funding shortfall and, in an unprecedented move, the presidents of the Royal Colleges of Surgeons, Physicians, and Obstetricians and Gynaecologists issued a joint statement claiming that the NHS had almost reached breaking point and that additional and alternative financing had to be provided.

Table 1: Annual growth in NHS spending.

Year	NHS Real growth (%)	NHS Volume growth (%)	HCHS* Real growth (%)	HCHS Volume growth (%)	FHS+ Real growth (%)	FHS Volume growth (%)
1978/79	1.5	2.2	1.1	2.5	9.7	7.8
1979/80	2.1	-0.7	2.3	-1.0	-0.2	-1.5
1980/81	9.8	2.6	11.5	3.0	4.9	1.4
1981/82	1.5	2.6	0.6	1.9	4.5	3.5
1982/83	2.0	4.1	0.6	1.1	7.5	6.3
1983/84	1.2	0.8	0.5	0.0	2.4	2.0
1984/85	2.0	1.0	0.7	-0.1	4.8	2.6
1985/86	0.2	0.5	0.0	0.6	0.4	0.9
1986/87	4.3	1.1	4.5	0.6	4.0	1.8
1987/88	5.0	2.4	4.9	1.9	5.3	3.7
1988/89	4.1	1.0	4.1	0.4	5.8	3.1
1989/90	-0.4	0.4	0.1	0.7	-2.6	-0.3
1990/91	3.8	3.5	3.8	3.2	2.7	0.9
1991/92	7.3	4.3	7.1	3.4	7.2	3.0
1992/93	5.7	4.1	5.7	2.9	6.2	5.7
1993/94	1.4	1.6	1.0	0.5**	2.8	4.8**
1994/95	3.0	2.0**	2.9	1.8**	4.9	3.9**
1995/96	2.9	2.8**	2.9	2.7**	2.2	2.0**
1996/97	0.9	0.7**	0.1	-0.1**	3.7	3.6**

Notes:* HCHS = Hospital and Community Health Services
     + FHS = Family Health Services
     ** = Estimates

Source: Dixon and Harrison (1997)

The government responded in two ways. First, in December 1987, Ministers announced that an extra £101 million was to be made available to the NHS in the UK to help tackle some of the immediate problems. Second, the Prime Minister decided to introduce a far reaching review of the future of the NHS. This decision was announced during an interview on the BBC TV programme, *Panorama*, in January 1988, and it was made clear that the results would be published within a year. The Prime Minister established and chaired a small committee of senior Ministers to undertake the review, which was supported by a group of civil servants and political advisors.

In fact, this was not the first occasion on which a review of the NHS had been undertaken. A working party comprising representatives of the Department of Health and Social Security, the Treasury, and the Health Departments of Wales, Scotland and Northern Ireland, together with two specialist advisors with experience of the private health care sector, had reported on alternative financing methods in 1982. As the Secretary of State at the time, Norman Fowler, explains in his memoirs, the government decided not to move away from a system in which the NHS was financed largely from taxation, on the basis of the working party's report. This was because other European countries were faced with similar problems to the UK and a centrally run and centrally funded health service like the NHS appeared to be most effective in controlling costs (Fowler, 1991).

In the absence of any specific proposals to change the basis of health service financing, Ministers pursued a policy of achieving greater efficiency in the NHS and encouraging the growth of private finance and provision alongside the NHS. The result was an expansion in the number of people covered by private health insurance schemes and in the role of private providers. By 1989, 13 per cent of the population in the UK was covered by private insurance. In parallel, the growth of private providers meant that by the end of the 1980s, eight per cent of all acute in-patients were treated privately and 17 per cent of all elective surgery was performed in the private sector. There was an even more rapid expansion of private residential and nursing home provision for elderly people and other vulnerable groups. Taken together, these changes meant that by the end of the decade private and voluntary hospitals and nursing homes supplied an estimated 15 per cent of all UK hospital based treatment and care by value (Laing, 1990).

The Ministerial Review

The Ministerial Review, initiated by Margaret Thatcher in 1988, offered an opportunity for alternative methods of financing and provision to be re-examined. The difficulty facing the government in this respect, as Norman Fowler indicates again, was that the NHS performed well when viewed in the international context. Total expenditure on health care, at around six per cent of GDP, was low by comparative standards, and yet for this spending the entire population had access to comprehensive services of a generally high standard. National planning meant that all parts of the country had access to health care, and a well developed system of primary care resulted in many medical problems being dealt with by GPs without the need to refer patients to hospitals. All this was achieved with only a small proportion of the budget being spent on administration (Ham, Robinson and Benzeval, 1990).

While problems clearly existed in relation to waiting lists for some treatments, poor quality of care provided for the so called priority groups, and lack of responsiveness to service users, they did not amount to a decisive case against the NHS. Rather, they indicated the need for a programme of reforms which retained the strengths of the NHS while the weaknesses were tackled. Indeed, for many of those who contributed to the debate, the most urgent requirement was extra money for the NHS to enable the changes that resulted from the *Griffiths Report* to be seen through. According to this school of thought, the key problem confronting the NHS was chronic and long term underfunding; there was nothing wrong with the structure of the NHS that additional resources would not overcome.

From this perspective, the control of health services spending exercised by the Treasury and seen by Norman Fowler as one of the strengths of the NHS, was in fact a major weakness in failing to deliver the volume of resources needed to fund the NHS to an adequate level. At a time when controlling public expenditure was an overriding political priority, it was not surprising that government Ministers were not persuaded by this argument, citing variations in performance across the NHS in support of their argument that existing budgets had to be used more efficiently before extra expenditure on the NHS could be justified (Lawson, 1992).

In its early stages the Ministerial Review focused on alternative methods for financing. This included looking again at the scope for increasing the role of private insurance and moving from tax funding to a social insurance system on the Western European model. Commenting on this aspect of the Review, Nigel Lawson notes in his memoirs:

> 'we looked . . . at other countries to see whether we could learn from them; but it was soon clear that every country we looked at was having problems with its provision of medical care. All of them − France, the United States, Germany − had different systems; but each of them had acute problems which none of them had solved. They were all in at least as much difficulty as we were, and it did not take long to conclude that there was surprisingly little that we could learn from any of the other systems. To try to change from the Health Service to any of the sorts of systems in use overseas would simply be out of the frying pan into the fire' (Lawson, 1992, p616).

The examination of alternative methods of financing was soon superseded by an analysis of how the delivery of services could be reformed, assuming the continuation of tax funding. It was on this basis that ideas put forward by an American economist, Alain Enthoven, caught the attention of Ministers.

In a report published in 1985, Enthoven argued that an internal market should be developed within the NHS and this idea was elaborated by a number of right-wing think-tanks in their input to the Review (Enthoven, 1985). The contribution of Enthoven's thinking was later acknowledged by Kenneth Clarke who said that he liked Enthoven's idea of the internal market:

> 'because it tried to inject into a state-owned system some of the qualities of competition, choice, and measurement of quality that you get in well-run, private enterprise' (Roberts, 1990, p1385).

It was Clarke who played a major part in the final stages of the Review and who was responsible for presenting the government's proposals following publication of the white paper, *Working for Patients*, in January 1989 (Secretary of State for Health and others, 1989).

Working for Patients

In the white paper, the government announced that the basic principles on which the NHS was founded would be preserved. Funding would continue to be provided mainly out of taxation and there were no plans to extend charges to patients. Tax relief on private insurance premiums was to be made available to those aged over 60, at the Prime Minister's insistence and against the advice of her Chancellor of the Exchequer (Lawson, 1992), but the significance of this was more symbolic than real. For the vast majority of the population, the NHS would continue to be the provider of health care and the government promised that access to care would be based on need. This was later reiterated by a future Secretary of State, Virginia Bottomley, in a speech to the British Medical Association:

'the government's commitment to the fundamental principles of the NHS has not wavered one jot . . . During the
NHS Review, more radical actions were considered and
rejected. They were thrown aside because they were
incompatible with the sacrosanct principle of the NHS:
that the care and treatment that the service provides should
be available to any man, woman or child, on the basis of
clinical need, regardless of the ability to pay' (Department
of Health, 1993a).

The main changes in *Working for Patients* concerned the delivery of health services. These changes were intended to create the
conditions for competition between hospitals and other
providers. This was to be achieved through a separation of purchaser and provider roles; the creation of self-governing NHS
trusts to run hospitals and other services; the transformation of
district health authorities into purchasers of services for local
people; the opportunity for larger GP practices to become
purchasers of some hospital services for their patients as GP
fundholders; and the use of contracts or service agreements to
provide links between purchasers and providers.

Fundamental to these proposals was that money would
follow patients. This was intended to overcome the efficiency
trap facing hospitals and to provide a stronger incentive than
global budgets for hospitals to improve their performance.
Ministers argued that a system in which providers had to compete for patients and resources would act as a significant stimulus to increase efficiency and to produce greater responsiveness
to patients. The result would be a higher level of uncertainty on
the part of providers about the source of their income but it was
argued that this was necessary if the NHS was to tackle success-
fully the problems it faced.

These and other proposals were sketched in broad outline in
Working for Patients, reflecting the speed with which the white
paper had been produced. Subsequently, a series of working
papers were published by the Department of Health containing
more detail on different aspects of the proposed reforms.

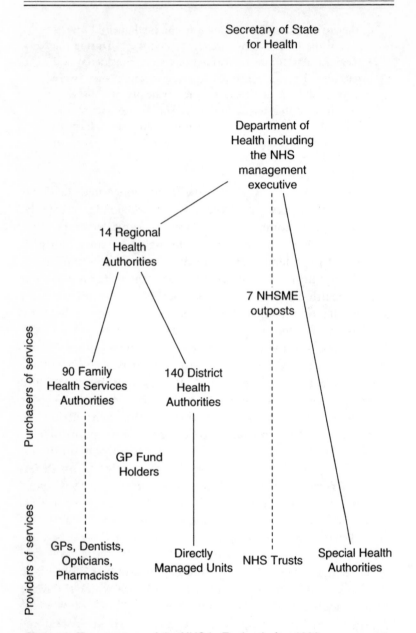

Figure 2: The structure of the NHS in England after 1990.

Together with the parallel changes to community care planned by the government, the proposals in *Working for Patients* were incorporated in the *NHS and Community Care Bill*. This was published in November 1989 and received the Royal Assent in June 1990, paving the way for the NHS market to come into operation from April 1991.

The debate about Working for Patients and the *NHS and Community Care Bill* aroused strong feelings on all sides (Ham, 1992a). Opposition to the government's proposals was led by the medical profession. The British Medical Association in particular opposed the introduction of market principles into health care. Organizations representing patients shared this concern as did bodies speaking for other professional and staff groups. There was more support for the reforms from managers and health authorities, although the timetable for implementing some of the changes was widely perceived to be unrealistic.

Figure 2 illustrates the organization of the NHS in England as it emerged after 1990. Unlike previous reorganizations, the structure did not change overnight and there was a progressive move away from the old to the new arrangements. Responsibility for overseeing the implementation of the reforms was vested in the NHS management executive working on behalf of Ministers. The management executive continued to be located within the Department of Health but increasingly it took on a separate existence from the policy divisions within the Department.

In this role, the management executive was used by Ministers to ensure that the reforms were implemented smoothly on the ground. The NHS Chief Executive, Duncan Nichol, assumed a higher profile as implementation gathered momentum, and attracted controversy in 1991 for supporting in public the policies of the government and appearing to criticize the opposition in the process. The NHS management executive worked increasingly with and through regional health authorities and sought to develop its role as the head office of the NHS. This was reinforced by the relocation of the management executive from London to Leeds in 1992.

Conclusion

The reforms to the NHS set out in *Working for Patients* were a response to acute funding problems that developed during the 1980s. Although the reforms in themselves did not tackle the long term underfunding of the NHS, they did seek to provide a way of ensuring that existing resources were used as efficiently as possible and that increases in productivity were rewarded and not penalized. More radical options for reform were considered and rejected during the Ministerial Review and it was for this reason that tax funding was retained. As Ministers emphasized, their proposals sought to preserve the founding principles of the NHS and to tackle the problems that existed by changes to the delivery of health services.

The logic behind this approach was that the NHS performed well when compared with other health care systems. To have proposed more fundamental reforms would have been to have put at risk the achievements of the NHS since 1948. Furthermore, from the Treasury's point of view, the great advantage of the NHS was its success in controlling overall levels of expenditure. Despite this, many of those involved in the NHS and a majority of the British public remained to be convinced that the proposals in *Working for Patients* would strengthen the NHS. The government's critics maintained that there was a hidden agenda behind the reforms and that the ultimate objective was to introduce a much higher level of private finance and private provision into the health sector. These are issues to which we return in the final chapter.

2 Implementing the NHS Reforms

The reforms introduced by the *NHS and Community Care Act* represent the biggest change to the delivery of health services since the inception of the NHS in 1948. Drawing on the ideas originally formulated by Alain Enthoven, it is often argued that the reforms involve the introduction of an internal market into the NHS. In fact, it is more accurate to use the phrase managed market. One reason for preferring this terminology is that competition is not confined to the NHS but also involves providers outside the NHS. Even more important is the fact that it has never been the government's intention to introduce a free market. Rather, the aim has been to graft some of the incentives that are often found in markets onto the structure of the NHS and to regulate or manage the operation of these incentives to avoid the problems of market failure.

The major developments in the implementation of the reforms are outlined in Box 1. As this shows, the reforms were implemented gradually over a period of years. *Working for Patients* contained proposals affecting almost all aspects of the NHS but the most significant elements of the reforms are:

☐ the separation of purchaser and provider roles;
☐ the creation of self-governing NHS trusts;
☐ the transformation of district health authorities into purchasers of services;
☐ the introduction of GP fundholding;
☐ the use of contracts or service agreements to provide links between purchasers and providers.

Taken together, the reforms involve a transition from an integrated system of health services financing and delivery to a contract system (OECD, 1992). They have proceeded in parallel with reforms of community care which are considered at the end of the chapter.

Box 1: The development of the NHS reforms.

1988

January — Margaret Thatcher announces Ministerial Review of the NHS.

July — Department of Health created following the splitting up of the Department of Health and Social Security. Kenneth Clarke appointed as Secretary of State for Health.

1989

January — *Working for Patients* published.

November — *NHS and Community Care Bill* published.

1990

June — *NHS and Community Care Bill* receives Royal Assent.

November — William Waldegrave replaces Kenneth Clarke as Secretary of State for Health.

1991

April — NHS reforms come into operation. The first wave of 57 NHS trusts and 306 GP fundholders is established in England.

October — The *Patient's Charter* published.

1992

April — The Conservative Party is re-elected. Virginia Bottomley replaces William Waldegrave as Secretary of State for Health. The second wave of 99 NHS trusts and 288 GP fundholders is established in England.

July — A white paper on *The Health of the Nation* is published.

October — The report of the *Tomlinson Inquiry* is published.

1993

February — The government publishes its response to the *Tomlinson Inquiry, Making London Better*.

A review of functions and manpower in the NHS is announced.

April — The third wave of 136 NHS trusts and over 600 GP fundholders is established in England.

July — The functions and manpower review reports to ministers.

October — The government publishes its response to the functions and manpower review, *Managing the New NHS*. This includes the proposed abolition of regional health authorities, the merger of district health authorities and family health services authorities, and a streamlining of the NHS management executive.

1994

April — The fourth wave of 140 NHS trusts and 800 GP fundholders is established in England. The NHS

Box 1: *continued*

	management executive is renamed the NHS executive and establishes eight regional offices. The number of regional health authorities is reduced from 14 to 8.
June	NHS performances tables published for the first time.
July	Department of Health publishes three reports setting out plans to streamline the role of the Department and the NHS executive.
October	*Developing NHS Purchasing and GP Fundholding* published.
November	*Health Authorities Bill* published.
December	*The Operation of the Internal Market: local freedoms, national responsibilities* published.

1995

January	An updated *Patient's Charter* published.
April	The fifth wave of 21 NHS trusts and 560 GP fund-holders is established in England. An accountability framework for fundholders is introduced.
June	*Health Authorities Bill* receives Royal Assent.
July	Stephen Dorrell replaces Virginia Bottomley as Secretary of State for Health
November	Plans to use private finance initiative to build new NHS hospitals announced.

1996

April	Regional health authorities are abolished and their functions taken over by NHS executive regional offices. District health authorities and family health services authorities replaced by unitary health authorities. The sixth wave of 1,200 GP fundholders is established in England. Around 50 total purchasing projects go live.
May	Efficiency scrutiny into burdens of paperwork published.
June	Consultation paper *Primary Care: the future* published.
October	A white paper on primary care, *Choice and Opportunity*, published. Reports of NHS funding problems.
November	A white paper on the future of the NHS, *The National Health Service. A Service with Ambitions*, published.
	The NHS (Primary Care) Bill published.
	Additional resources for the NHS announced.
December	A second white paper on primary care, *Primary Care: delivering the future*, published.

The Separation of Purchaser and Provider Roles

Before the reforms were introduced, district health authorities received a budget from regional health authorities to manage the hospital and community health services in their areas. These services were directly managed by district health authorities who had a statutory duty to keep within budget and were responsible for maintaining appropriate standards of care. The cost of treating patients who used these services but lived outside the area was allowed for in the budget setting process. This was achieved by regional health authorities adjusting for the flow of patients across district boundaries and allocating resources to district health authorities accordingly. As a consequence, district health authorities were funded primarily to provide services in the hospital and community health services that they managed.

This was reflected in the way in which district health authorities carried out their responsibilities. For the most part, district health authorities were intent on expanding and improving health services in their areas and responding to the demands of those involved in service provision. It was this that led many researchers to conclude that the NHS was provider dominated and that district health authorities had been captured by providers to the detriment of other interests. The separation of purchaser and provider roles was in part intended to challenge provider dominance and to give greater attention to the needs of patients and the public.

It was also designed to break the strong link that existed between district health authorities and their local providers in order to encourage district health authorities to purchase services from other providers where this offered benefits to patients. In this way, providers would be put in the position of having to compete for contracts from purchasers. Instead of being funded to provide services in their hospitals, district health authorities are now allocated resources to buy services for the people who live in their area. This means that district health authority budgets are no longer adjusted for cross boundary patient flows but are based solely on the size of the population weighted for age, sex and other factors.

The architects of the reforms believed that competition would stimulate providers to increase their efficiency and to improve quality. This was to be achieved by creating a system in which money followed the patient. This principle was designed to overcome the efficiency trap which existed before the reforms in which providers were in effect penalized for treating more patients because their income did not increase in line with productivity. The obverse was that in the new system inefficient providers would be penalized if they were not able to attract contracts and resources from purchasers. These providers would then be forced to improve their performance or risk going out of business. This held out a quite different prospect from the old NHS in which hospitals only closed as a result of planned changes in service provision. In this respect, the logic of the reforms was inescapable: the introduction of competition in to a health service in which the budget was fixed meant that winners had to be matched by losers (Ham, 1989).

The separation of purchaser and provider roles did not happen immediately across the NHS. Rather, there was a gradual process of change in which initially the main priority was to clarify management responsibilities within district health authorities. This involved devolving responsibility for providing services to the unit level of management, leaving the staff at district health authority headquarters to take on the purchasing role. These changes resulted in a considerable reduction in the number of staff employed in district health authorities. This applied particularly to functions such as finance, human resources and estates, where there was almost complete devolution of staff and responsibility to units. As a consequence, a small core of staff remained at district level and they combined responsibility for purchasing with oversight of the performance of units.

A variety of management arrangements were put in place to achieve a separation of roles within district health authorities.

These arrangements reflected the fact that district health authorities continued to carry statutory responsibility for directly managed units until they became NHS trusts and they therefore had to maintain an interest in the affairs of directly managed units. In this situation, district health authorities were characterized as 'holding on while letting go', having to ensure that directly managed units balanced their budgets and maintained appropriate standards of care while preparing these units to become self-governing organizations (Ham, 1990b).

Given that separation of roles was incomplete, and that district health authorities were responsible for any financial problems that occurred within their directly managed units, there was little incentive for district health authorities to move contracts from these units to other providers. To have done so would have created more difficulties than it would have solved because district health authorities would have had to deal with the consequences of budget shortfalls in their units. Any improvements in efficiency or quality achieved in this way would have been offset by the challenge of bringing capacity at local units into line with available resources.

It followed that initially competition was tightly constrained. It became clear that the development of a market in health services was contingent on a complete separation of purchaser and provider roles and the transfer of a majority of directly managed units to NHS trusts. Only in this way would district health authorities be able to become pure purchasers and reach independent decisions on where contracts should be placed.

NHS Trusts

The first NHS trusts were established on 1 April 1991. On that day 57 trusts came in to existence covering a range of services. These included acute hospitals, community services, mental health, learning difficulties, ambulance services and a combination of all of these services. Whereas *Working for Patients* had indicated that trust status would be available as an option for acute hospitals with more than 250 beds, in practice all services became eligible and it was quickly made clear that trust status was the preferred model for provider units. Accordingly, a further 99 trusts were established in 1992, followed by 136 in 1993. Most of the remaining units achieved trust status in 1994 with the effect that almost all services were managed by trusts.

During 1992 the Department of Health made clear that it expected applications for trust status not to combine acute and community services. This reflected a concern that had emerged in London where there was evidence to suggest that in combined trusts budgetary deficits in acute services were tackled by taking money from community services. At a time when government policy was seeking to give greater priority to community services, establishing separate trusts for the management of these services was seen as a way of protecting their budgets. This policy was not, however, applied retrospectively, and trusts established in the first and second waves were not required to split acute services and community services.

Trusts were established on the basis that they would have a number of freedoms not available to directly managed units. These freedoms were of three types: financial, personnel and managerial. *Working for Patients* had indicated that trusts would have a degree of flexibility in borrowing money, enabling them to raise capital from private sources as well as the Treasury. In practice, this flexibility was largely illusory. Guidance issued by the Department of Health required trusts to borrow on the best terms available and in effect this meant borrowing from the Treasury. Furthermore, the amount that trusts could spend on capital developments was constrained by external financing limits set each year by the Department of Health. In practical terms, therefore, the financial freedoms of trusts were shackled by traditional public sector rules.

There was much greater freedom in relation to personnel where trusts were no longer constrained by national Whitley Council pay rates and terms of service but were able to negotiate locally with their staff. A number of trusts used this freedom to change the position of staff but in general movement in this direction was slow (IRS Employment Trends, 1993). Given the size of the NHS workforce, and the extent of the effort involved in renegotiating employment contracts, most trusts chose to make changes step by step and avoided any major departures from past practice.

As a consequence, the management freedoms of trusts were more significant than the changes in the financial regime and personnel policy. In particular, the ability of trusts to manage their affairs as self-governing institutions, without having to report through district and regional health authorities, was an important innovation. The effect was to liberate managers and health care professionals to make much needed improvements in service provision. In this situation, trusts were held accountable primarily via the contracts they negotiated with purchasers rather than through the old line management relationship with the district health authority.

Alongside accountability through contracts, there grew up an arrangement whereby the performance of trusts was monitored by the NHS management executive. At first, this was done on a national basis, but the establishment of 156 trusts from April 1992 led to the creation of six (later seven) outposts of the man-agement executive organized on a regional basis. Each outpost employed a small number of staff with the majority of the staff coming from financial backgrounds. The outposts were respon-sible for monitoring the financial performance of trusts, agree-ing with them an external financing limit, and approving their business plans each year. Any suggestion that trusts should be held accountable through regional health authorities was strongly resisted by trust chairmen and chief executives who wanted to avoid being drawn back in to what they perceived as old style, bureaucratic controls. In order to protect trusts, the Secretary of State for Health wrote to the chairman of the Mersey Regional Health Authority in 1991 to emphasize that trusts did not come under the ambit of regional health authorities.

There thus emerged two kinds of agency at the intermediate tier of NHS management: management executive outposts, responsible for monitoring the performance of NHS trusts; and regional health authorities, given the job of overseeing the work of district health authorities and family health services authorities and managing the purchasing function. The future of the intermediate tier was reviewed as part of the Functions and Manpower Review established in 1993. The proposal within the Review to abolish regional health authorities led ultimately to the integration of the functions of management executive outposts and regional health authorities (*see* below), although the monitoring of performance of NHS trusts continued to be on a light touch basis.

District Health Authorities as Purchasers

The gradual establishment of NHS trusts, emerging like butterflies from the shell of a chrysalis, had the effect of slowing down the development of the new role of district health authorities as purchasers. Since much of the history and experience of district health authorities had focused on providers, there was a natural inclination on the part of managers working in district health authorities to continue to take a close interest in this side of the NHS. This was reinforced by the relative neglect of the purchaser role by Ministers and the management executive. In the early stages of the reforms, priority was attached to the establishment of NHS trusts and GP fundholders, and as a result it took some time before the full significance of the new function of district health authorities was recognized.

What support there was for district health authorities was focused nationally on *Project 26* (later renamed the *District Health Authority Project*) in the NHS management executive. This was a project which brought together 11 district health authorities from different parts of the country to share their experience of purchasing and to distil the lessons for dissemination across the NHS. In parallel, *Project 26* initiated a number of studies into how other district health authorities were taking on their responsibilities, and it commissioned a series of health needs assessment reports as a resource for purchasers. The result of all of this activity was a range of publications bringing together accumulated knowledge of purchasing (NHSME 1989, 1990, 1991, 1992).

Greater priority was attached to purchasing following the appointment of William Waldegrave as Secretary of State for Health and Andrew Foster as Deputy Chief Executive of the NHS management executive. Compared with their predecessors, both Waldegrave and Foster recognized the importance of purchasing and saw the establishment of an effective purchasing function as the key to making the reforms work. In particular, purchasers were seen as central to the successful implementation of the government's national health strategy. This emerged in a green paper in 1991 and a white paper, *The Health of Nation*, in 1992 (*see* Box 2). The strategy outlined a series of targets for improving the health of the population and Ministers made it clear that they saw purchasers as having the lead responsibility for delivering that strategy.

To help in the development of purchasing, £10 million was set aside nationally by Ministers in February 1992. This was reinforced in 1993, when the new Ministerial team at the Department of Health, led by Virginia Bottomley, gave a series of speeches in which they emphasized the significance of purchasing and maintained that purchasers had the major responsibility to drive ahead with the reforms. The lead in this area was taken by the Minister of State for Health, Brian Mawhinney, whose support for purchasing grew out of experience of bringing about changes in hospital services in London. At a time when the hospitals affected were universally critical of government policy, Mawhinney was impressed by the support he received from purchasers in London and their willingness to work with the government to achieve change. A further £4 million was earmarked nationally in 1993 as a resource for purchaser development.

Box 2: The Health of the Nation.

Coronary Heart Disease (CHD) and Stroke
- to reduce death rates for both CHD and stroke in people under 65 by at least 40 per cent by the year 2000 (Baseline 1990)

- to reduce the death rate for CHD in people aged 65–74 by at least 30 per cent by the year 2000 (Baseline 1990)

- to reduce the death rate for stroke in people aged 65–74 by at least 40 per cent by the year 2000 (Baseline 1990)

Cancers
- to reduce the death rate for breast cancer in the population invited for screening by at least 25 per cent by the year 2000 (Baseline 1990)

- to reduce the incidence of invasive cervical cancer by at least 20 per cent by the year 2000 (Baseline 1990)

- to reduce the death rate for lung cancer under the age of 75 by at least 30 per cent in men and by at least 15 per cent in women by 2010 (Baseline 1990)

- to halt the year-on-year increase in the incidence of skin cancer by 2005

Mental Illness
- to improve significantly the health and social functioning of mentally ill people

- to reduce the overall suicide rate by at least 15 per cent by the year 2000 (Baseline 1990)

- to reduce the suicide rate of severely mentally ill people by at least 33 per cent by the year 2000 (Baseline 2000)

HIV/AIDS and Sexual Health
- to reduce the incidence of gonorrhoea by at least 20 per cent by 1995 (Baseline 1990) as an indicator of HIV/AIDS trends

- to reduce by at least 50 per cent the rate of conceptions amongst the under-16s by the year 2000 (Baseline 1989)

Accidents
- to reduce the death rate for accidents among children aged under 15 by at least 33 per cent by 2005 (Baseline 1990)

- to reduce the death rate for accidents among young people aged 15–24 by at least 25 per cent by 2005 (Baseline 1990)

- to reduce the death rate for accidents among people aged 65 and over by at least 33 per cent by 2005 (Baseline 1990).

One of the consequences of the establishment of NHS trusts was that proposals were put forward to merge district health authorities. There were a number of reasons for this, including the shortage of managers with skills in purchasing, the fact that some district health authorities were too small to form viable purchasing organizations, the greater financial leverage available to bigger district health authorities, and a desire to achieve coterminosity with other agencies, particularly family health services authorities and local authorities (Ham and Heginbotham, 1991). As mergers proceeded, many district health authorities sought to avoid the dangers of remoteness and insensitivity by setting up purchasing arrangements that were sensitive to the needs of small areas or localities (Ham, 1992b).

Correspondingly, district health authorities and family health services authorities engaged in joint working of various kinds. In a number of regions, this resulted in the creation of health commissions and similar agencies. These agencies involved district health authorities and family health services authorities developing joint management arrangements (Ham, Schofield and Williams, 1993). Following the report of the Functions and Manpower Review, ministers brought forward legislation to integrate the responsibilities of the two types of authority, and this change eventually took effect in 1996.

In this context, the different approach taken by district health authorities and GP fundholders to purchasing in some parts of the country became a concern. With fundholders buying a defined range of services for their patients, and district health authorities purchasing the remaining services and the full range of care for the patients of non-fundholders, there was a risk of harmful instability if the plans of the two types of purchaser were not coordinated. In areas where district health authorities and fundholders worked together this was not a problem, but elsewhere it was difficult to see how the idea of a district general hospital providing a comprehensive range of services for a given population could be sustained when individual purchasers were intent on shopping around for the best deal for their patients.

It was partly for this reason that ministers introduced an accountability framework for fundholders in 1995 designed to ensure that a mechanism was in place for co-ordinating the plans of health authorities and fundholders.

GP Fundholding

The first GP fundholders took responsibility for their budgets on 1 April 1991. On that day, 306 practices were established, involving GPs in England and covering seven per cent of the population. As with NHS trusts, more GP fundholders entered the scheme on an annual basis thereafter. By 1996 there were 3,735 practices in the scheme in England involving 13,400 GPs and covering over 50 per cent of the population. The expansion of fundholding in England is illustrated in Figure 3.

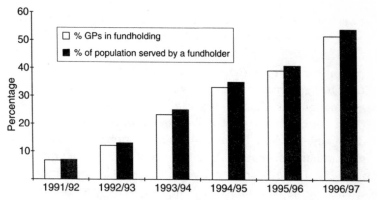

Figure 3: The development of GP fundholding.

The rules on GP fundholding evolved in the light of experience. Whereas *Working for Patients* had specified that only practices with 11,000 patients or more would be eligible to apply to become fundholders, this list size was progressively reduced to 9,000 and then to 7,000 and eventually 5,000. At the same time, smaller practices were encouraged to become fundholders by linking up with each other and with larger practices in what became known as multifunds. Initially, the fundholding scheme enabled GPs to purchase a defined range of service for their patients (*see* Box 3). These services included most outpatient treatment and elective surgery, diagnostic tests and investigations, drugs and appliances, and staff employed in the practice such as receptionists and nurses. In 1993 the scope of the scheme was widened to encompass a number of community services. These services comprised district nursing and health visiting, chiropody, physiotherapy and dietetics, and some services for people with mental illness and learning disabilities. Fundholders were therefore responsible for purchasing around 20 per cent of hospital and community health services for their patients by value, the remainder being purchased by the district health authority.

Figures published by the Audit Commission illustrate the composition of fundholders' budgets. In 1994/95 a typical fundholder was responsible for a budget of about £1.7 million or £160 for each patient on the practice list. Of this sum, £780,000 was available to purchase hospital and mental health care, £660,000 to cover the cost of drugs, £160,000 for community nursing and health visiting, and £115,000 for practice staff (Audit Commission, 1995). *Working for Patients* had envisaged that budgets would be based on a capitation formula. This was subsequently dropped in favour of a formula based on the use practices made of the services contained in the fundholding scheme in the past and their cost. One of the consequences was wide variations in the budgets allocated to fundholders. While most practices had between £140 and £170 to spend for each patient on their lists, at the extremes there were threefold variations in the budgets available per patient (Audit Commission, 1995).

To help GPs take on the responsibility of holding a budget, practices received additional funding in the year in which they prepared to become fundholders. They also received an annual

Box 3: The growth of GP fundholding.

Originally, the scheme included the following services:

Hospital services: a defined range of elective operative procedures; outpatient services; diagnostic tests and investigations.

Prescribing expenditure: drugs and appliances.

Practice staff: the cost of employing staff such as nurses and receptionists

In 1993 the following services were added:

Health visiting and district nursing.

Dietetic and chiropody services.

Mental health out-patient and community services and health services for people with learning difficulties.

Mental health counselling.

Referrals made by health visitors, district nurses, community psychiatric nurses and community mental handicap nurses.

In 1996 fundholding was further developed with three options available:

Community fundholding for practices with 3,000 patients or more, covering practice staff, drugs, diagnostic tests and some community services.

Standard fundholding for practices with 5,000 patients or more, expanded to include virtually all elective surgery, out-patients and community services.

Total purchasing in which around 50 pilot projects purchased all hospital and community health services for their patients. This built on four earlier initiatives and was extended to another 30 projects in 1997.

---

management allowance on becoming fundholders in recognition of the staff and equipment costs incurred. To begin with the size of the management allowance was the same for all practices but from 1995 it was based on the size of the practice list, the number of branch surgeries, and the number of practices in the fund. For a practice of 11,000 patients and surgeries on two sites, the maximum allowance available was £47,500. With these additional funds, practices employed fund managers and other staff to deal with the workload involved.

Practices were safeguarded against the cost of expensive patients by an arrangement under which fundholders were only liable for the first £5,000 of treatment for any one patient each year. This was later increased to £6,000. Analysis demonstrates that most practices underspent their budgets in the early years of the scheme with savings amounting to £64 million or 3.5 per cent of the total in 1993/94. There were, however, considerable variations between practices, with 20 per cent of practices saving £100,000 or more and three per cent overspending by that amount (Audit Commission, 1995). While the rules laid down by the Department of Health were meant to prohibit GPs from benefiting personally from savings, they were able to use savings to improve their premises and in this way they did gain financially. Perhaps not surprisingly, improvements to premises was the most popular use of savings, followed by the purchase of furnishings and office equipment and medical equipment.

In the early stages, one of the most controversial aspects of fundholding was the decision of some practices to set up private companies to provide services. This was a way of getting around the rules that practices were not allowed to use their resources to buy services from themselves. In 1993, new guidance was issued forbidding fundholders from establishing private companies. As a *quid pro quo*, the rules were relaxed to enable GPs in fundholding practices to be paid for providing some services outside the scope of their existing contract such as diagnostic testing and minor surgery, subject to the approval of regional health authorities.

Research into the impact of fundholding demonstrated that GPs in fundholding practices brought about a number of changes in service provision. These included employing a wider range of staff in the practice, negotiating shorter waiting times for hospital services, switching contracts between providers where improved services were available, and reviewing prescribing patterns to obtain better value for money in the use of the drugs budget (Glennerster *et al.*, 1992 and 1994). On this last point, the evidence indicated that fundholding had proved more effective in curbing increases in prescribing costs than indicative prescribing (Bradlow and Coulter, 1993). This was of particular interest to the Treasury given the rapid increase in prescribing costs during this period and the absence of cash limits in this area of expenditure.

Supporters of the reforms cited these changes in service provision to argue that fundholders were at the leading edge of the reforms and were achieving greater success as purchasers than district health authorities. Against this, it should be noted that the practices included in the scheme initially were among the best organized and managed in the country, and the process of setting budgets in some cases erred in favour of GPs. Furthermore, district health authorities were constrained by their continuing responsibility for directly managed units and the emphasis placed by Ministers on the gradual and planned implementation of the reforms. In these circumstances, it would have been surprising if some fundholders had not demonstrated greater initiative than district health authorities.

From the public's point of view, the most significant aspect of fundholding was the quicker access to hospitals enjoyed by the patients of fundholders compared with those of non-fundholders. Claims of a two-tier service surfaced very quickly after the introduction of the reforms and led to the government agreeing guidelines with the medical profession on priorities for treatment. These guidelines were framed in such a way as to be incomprehensible to most people. This was probably deliberate, enabling as it did a variety of interpretations to be placed on the guidelines.

In the light of this, it was hardly surprising that the British Medical Association was able to show, in a report published in 1993, that fundholders' patients continued to receive preferential treatment. The reforms made it inevitable that purchasing power would determine access to care rather than clinically defined need. Notwithstanding concerns that the principle of equity on which the NHS was based was being undermined, the British Medical Association dropped its opposition to fundholding, largely as a pragmatic response to the decision of an increasing number of GPs to become fundholders.

In 1994 the Department of Health published a review of the development of purchasing and the future of fundholding. This led to the further expansion of the standard fundholding scheme and the introduction of two new options: total purchasing in which GPs were able to buy all services for their patients; and community fundholding in which practices with 3,000 patients or more purchased practice staff, drugs, diagnostic tests and community health services. Both options came into operation in 1996. In parallel, the Department of Health emphasized that there was a continuing role for health authorities as strategic commissioning bodies. This included working with GPs not involved in fundholding to ensure that their needs were reflected in health authority purchasing decisions.

In this context, it should be noted that alongside fundholding there emerged a variety of other ways of involving GPs in purchasing decisions. These ranged from GP involvement in district health authority purchasing, the development of locality-sensitive purchasing, and practice-sensitive purchasing (see Figure 4). A wide variety of initiatives were taken across the NHS and many GPs preferred to influence purchasing through these initiatives rather than by holding a budget directly. This was demonstrated by figures showing wide variations in fundholding coverage, ranging from 84 per cent of GPs being involved in fundholding in some districts to only four per cent in others in 1995. Partly because of this, it became clear that fundholding, unlike NHS trust status, would not become universal. Rather, there would be a mixture of methods for enabling GPs to influence purchasing decisions and no one model would apply in all places.

Contracts

NHS contracts provide the link between purchasers and providers. At an early stage, the government made it clear that contracts were not legal documents. In view of this, they are more accurately described as service agreements. The purpose of

Figure 4: Spectrum of options for GP involvement in purchasing.

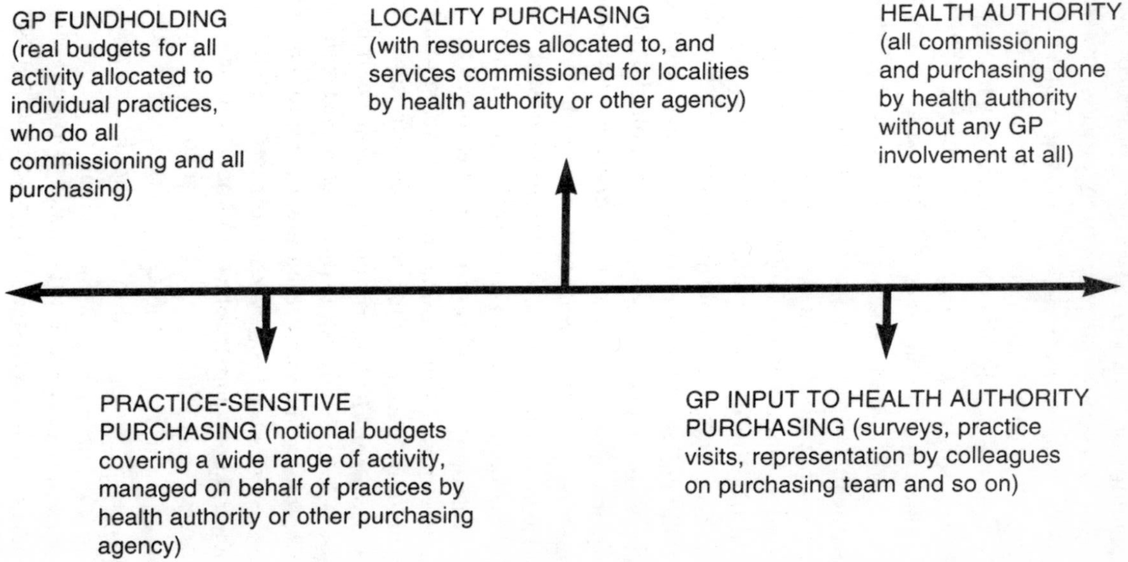

GP FUNDHOLDING
(real budgets for all
activity allocated to
individual practices,
who do all
commissioning and all
purchasing)

LOCALITY PURCHASING
(with resources allocated to, and
services commissioned for localities
by health authority or other agency)

HEALTH AUTHORITY
(all commissioning
and purchasing done
by health authority
without any GP
involvement at all)

PRACTICE-SENSITIVE
PURCHASING (notional budgets
covering a wide range of activity,
managed on behalf of practices by
health authority or other purchasing
agency)

GP INPUT TO HEALTH AUTHORITY
PURCHASING (surveys, practice
visits, representation by colleagues
on purchasing team and so on)

contracts, or service agreements, is to specify the cost, quality and quantity of care that should be provided. Contracts are made at the end of the purchasing process and set down in writing the range of services that NHS trusts and other providers have agreed to deliver to their purchasers.

Guidance issued by the Department of Health shortly after publication of *Working for Patients* envisaged that contracts would be of three main types: block, cost and volume, and cost per case (*see* Box 4). To begin with, most contracts negotiated by district health authorities were block contracts. These involved purchasers paying providers an agreed sum of money over a period of a year to deliver a defined range of services. Payments were usually made on a monthly basis and were tied to the provision of a certain workload during the year. For the most part, this workload was based on previous patterns of treatment and was expressed in general terms, for example the total number of in-patients, out-patients and day cases.

Cost and volume contracts involved purchasers paying an agreed price to deliver a specified volume of work. Any variation in the volume of work attracted additional payments or deductions as appropriate. Cost and volume contracts tended to be favoured by district health authorities placing smaller contracts and by GP fundholders. Cost per case contracts were even more popular among GP fundholders and were used by both fundholders and district health authorities to pay for the treatment of individual cases not covered by other forms of contracts.

One of the most controversial features of contracting was the use of extra contractual referrals. These were referrals made by GPs to hospitals which did not have a contract with the district health authority where the GP practised. If these referrals fell outside the terms of fundholding, the district health authority was responsible for approving them and agreeing to make payments. Under the rules laid down by the Department of Health, emergency extra contractual referrals had to be dealt with immediately and the cost met in full by the relevant district health authority. The same applied to tertiary referrals, that is

Box 4: Different types of contract.

Type	Definition
Simple block	Purchasers pay the provider a fixed sum for access to a defined range of services or facilities. Such contracts may include some form of indicative workload agreement or fixed volume.
Sophisticated block	Purchasers pay providers a fixed contract sum for access to a defined range of services or facilities. Indicative patient activity targets or thresholds with 'floors' and 'ceilings' are included in such contracts as well as agreed mechanisms if targets are exceeded. Some elements of case-mix may be included.
Cost and volume	This contract specifies outputs in terms of patient treatment rather than inputs in terms of services or facilities available. Purchasers do not purchase fixed volumes but will develop contracts with a fixed price being paid up to a certain volume of treatment and a price per case being paid above it, up to a volume ceiling.
Cost per case	The hospital agrees to provide a range of specified treatments in line with a given contract price.

Source: Purchasing Unit, NHS Executive

referrals made by one consultant to another. On the other hand, elective extra contractual referrals had to be approved in advance by the district health authority following a GP's request.

This required district health authorities to establish procedures for handling extra contractual referrals and for determining how much money should be set aside for this purpose. In some cases, this involved negotiating with GPs as to whether the referral was necessary. In other cases, particularly where budgets were tight, it meant refusing to approve extra contractual referrals or delaying them until the following financial year, thereby limiting the freedom of choice of GPs and patients. In practice, difficulties of this kind arose only in a small proportion of cases, but it was nevertheless an issue on which many GPs and patients felt strongly. The administration of extra contractual referrals was also costly and time consuming (Ghodse, 1995). In recognition of this, proposals were put forward in 1996 for simplifying the procedures for handling elective extra contractual referrals following an efficiency scrutiny into NHS paperwork.

As purchasers and providers gained experience of contracting, the Department of Health encouraged movement away from simple block contracts to more sophisticated arrangements. Survey evidence indicated that this was indeed happening as health authorities negotiated contracts which were a hybrid of simple block contracts and cost and volume contracts. This included agreeing extra payments for increases in activity, often on the basis of marginal prices (Raftery *et al.*, 1996). There was also a tendency to move towards contracts over a period of more than a year and to use competitive tendering for some clinical services (Appleby, 1994 and 1995). Notwithstanding these developments, a study by the National Audit Office highlighted the inadequacies of contracting for acute services and the need to improve information systems to support contracting (National Audit Office, 1995). The development of more sophisticated contracts was hampered by these inadequacies as well as by the cost of introducing new systems to fill the gaps in data that existed.

There was also a reluctance on the part of some purchasers to assume the risks involved in more sophisticated contracts. Block contracts were undoubtedly a crude tool but they at least had the virtue from a purchaser's point of view of controlling expenditure. The greater use of sophisticated contracts in which planned increases in activity triggered additional payments for providers created more uncertainty for purchasers and the risk that their budgets would be overspent. Given the absence of reliable information on case mix, there was also a danger that unscrupulous providers would 'game' the system to their advantage by maximizing the throughput of simple cases at the expense of those that were more complex. In view of the lack of tried and tested methods for monitoring contract compliance, many purchasers were reluctant to expose themselves to this danger.

The difficulty this created for providers was that increases in activity were not rewarded with increases in income. In other words, the efficiency trap which gave rise to the NHS reforms continued to cause problems. Providers that fulfilled their contracts ahead of schedule were forced to postpone elective admissions until their new contracts came into operation. As a number of observers pointed out, far from money following the patients, the patients were required to follow the money associated with block contracts (Ham, 1992c).

In this situation, the incentives to improve performance that the reforms were supposed to introduce were not much in evidence. The response of Ministers was to urge providers to manage their workload more effectively throughout the year and to ensure that clinicians were involved fully in contract negotiations. This achieved some success in avoiding hospitals having to stop admissions part way through the year but the underlying problem of a health service in which there was a mismatch between resource allocation and activity remained. Despite these problems, there were a number of examples of good practice in contracting. These were highlighted in a report from the management executive published in 1993. Examples drawn from the report are displayed in Box 5.

One of the concerns expressed at the inception of the reforms was that quality would be sacrificed by purchasers in the pursuit of increased activity and lower prices. Evidence from the use of contracts indicates that a wide range of quality standards were specified by purchasers, covering such issues as waiting times, patient satisfaction, and a requirement to undertake medical audit. Much less attention was paid to standards of clinical quality. This reflects largely the absence of data on clinical quality and the difficulty of comparing providers on a consistent basis. Publication of the *Patient's Charter* in October 1991 (*see* Box 6) ensured that the emphasis continued to be placed on issues of access and patient convenience. The publication of league tables of the performance of providers based on the *Patient's Charter* beginning in 1994 meant that these aspects of quality received

Box 5: Good practice in contracting.

Salford District Health Authority was planning to use `block plus' contracts with its top ten providers in 1994/95. These contracts would have floor and ceiling levels within five per cent of the target volume of activity. Additional payments would be made at marginal costs.

The West Midlands Regional Health Authority and its district health authorities used a regional specialties agency to negotiate contracts for regional specialties. The rationale for this is that specialties with high costs and low volumes require a different approach from other services. The agency acts on behalf of all district health authorities in the region to purchase regional specialty services from designated units.

Four health commissions in the Wessex region collaborated over the pro-duction of a common set of quality specifications for inclusion in contracts. This included an approach to monitoring, involving annual visits to all providers, quality reports and information from GPs.

The Mersey Regional Health Authority developed a system of incentives to reduce waiting times for treatment. Bonus payments are made to providers who achieve the regional target of no patient waiting longer than 12 months. Where a provider fails to meet the target, the district health authority is encouraged to claw back waiting time funds and invest them elsewhere.

---

even greater prominence. In recognition of this, Ministers used publication of NHS performance tables in 1996 to announce that they were examining the scoping for including measures of clinical standards in future years.

A number of issues relating to contracts were reviewed in the first reports to be published by the Clinical Standards Advisory Group. The government agreed to set up this Group during the debate on the *NHS and Community Care Bill*, in response to representations from the medical profession that there should be an independent source of expert advice to the UK Health Ministers and the NHS on standards of clinical care. Initially, the Clinical Standards Advisory Group reviewed arrangements made for four services: neonatal intensive care, cystic fibrosis, childhood leukaemia, and coronary artery bypass grafting and angiography. In a wide ranging review, the Group concluded that

Box 6: The Patient's Charter.

Ten rights were included in the *Patient's Charter* published in 1991. These are:

- to receive health care on the basis of clinical need, regardless of ability to pay;

- to be registered with a GP;

- to receive emergency medical care at any time through a GP or through emergency ambulance service and hospital accident and emergency department;

- to be referred to a consultant, acceptable to a patient, when a GP thinks this necessary and to be referred for a second opinion if a patient and GP agree this to be desirable;

- to be given a clear explanation of any treatment proposed, including any risks or alternatives;

- to have access to health records, and to know that those working for the NHS are under a legal duty to keep their contents confidential;

- to choose whether or not to take part in medical research or medical student training;

- to be given detailed information on local health services, including quality standards and maximum waiting times;

- to be guaranteed admission for treatment by a specific date no later than two years from the day when a patient is placed on a waiting list;

- to have any complaint about NHS services investigated and to receive a full and prompt written reply from the chief executive or general manager.

The updated and enlarged *Patient's Charter* published in 1995 set out new rights and standards including:

- 90 per cent of out-patients to be seen within 13 weeks for their first appointment and everyone within 26 weeks;

- all patients waiting for an operation to be guaranteed admission for treatment no later than 18 months from the day of being placed on a waiting list;

- a three to four hour standard for 'trolley waits' in accident and emergency departments, to be reduced to two hours from April 1996;

- urgent home visits by community nurses within four hours and for non-urgent patients within two days.

contracting was taking place in a rudimentary fashion, that contracts were too crude an instrument to be used in purchasing specialized services, and professional staff had been insufficiently involved in the preparation of contracts. The Group also argued that individual district health authorities did not always have the expertise needed to purchase these specialist services and collaboration between health authorities might be needed in future. The Group concluded that issues concerned with clinical quality had been largely ignored (Clinical Standards Advisory Group, 1993). In response, the Department of Health issued revised guidance to health authorities on contracting for specialist services.

Community Care

In parallel with the reforms to the NHS, the government introduced major changes to the financing and delivery of community care. These changes stemmed from the white paper, *Caring for People*, which was itself a response to a report prepared by Sir Roy Griffiths in 1988. Both documents acknowledged that progress in developing services in the community for vulnerable groups, such as the frail elderly and the mentally ill, had been patchy. Furthermore, there was an incentive to admit people to residential care in the community, for example nursing homes, rather than to provide support in people's own homes. This was because residential care was funded through the social security budget and had to be provided to individuals who met the requirements for income support. The existence of this entitlement meant that expenditure on this part of the social security budget increased rapidly during the 1980s. The reforms set out in *Caring for People* were intended to halt the rise in expenditure, remove the incentive to use residential care, and ensure that a wider range of services was available to those in need.

The provisions of *Caring for People* were incorporated in the *NHS and Community Care Act* of 1990. The Act gave local authorities the lead responsibility for community care and their role was that of enablers rather than direct service providers. Local authorities were required to prepare community care plans in association with health authorities and other agencies. They were also given additional resources to enable them to discharge their responsibilities. Most of these resources involved the transfer of funds from the social security budget. The government made it clear that it expected these funds to be used primarily to buy services from providers in the independent sector rather than to fund direct provision by local authorities. This meant that a community care market began to grow alongside the NHS market based on a separation of purchaser and provider roles, the use of contracts, and the emergence of a mixed economy of care.

The original intention was that the changes to community care would be implemented at the same time as the reforms of the NHS. In the event, the government delayed implementing the transfer of funds to local authorities until 1993 because of difficulties that had arisen over the community charge, or poll tax. Local authorities used the intervening period to prepare themselves for the new arrangements, including making provision for the assessment of individuals' needs for care. The principal responsibility for needs assessment rested with care managers employed by local authorities. Care managers were expected to work with GPs and other colleagues from the NHS to determine what services were required.

In 1993/94, £399 million was transferred from the social security budget to local authorities as the first stage in implementing the community care reforms. These resources were ring-fenced to ensure that they were indeed used for this purpose. At the same time, the government provided a further £140 million, in recognition of the additional costs that local authorities incurred as a result of the changes. The associations representing local authorities argued that these sums fell short of what was required and would mean that not all needs could be met. This gave rise to concerns that some individuals might receive no services at all, even though they had been assessed as in need, while others would be cared for in inappropriate settings. In particular, health authorities feared that acute hospital beds might be blocked by elderly people ready to be discharged but for whom no alternative services were available.

In practice, monitoring undertaken by the Department of Health concluded that the new community care arrangements had got off to a broadly satisfactory start. This was confirmed by the Audit Commission in its reviews. Although implementation was slower than in the case of the NHS reforms, and while there was little enthusiasm on the part of some local authorities for the principles of competition and contracting, progress had been made in putting in place arrangements for assessing needs and commissioning services. This in turn had led to the development of alternatives to residential care. Against this, there were continuing concerns about the impact of resource constraints which led many authorities to tighten eligibility criteria in order to keep within budget and target resources on those in greatest need.

In the broader context, the community care reforms highlighted the importance of priority setting or rationing. The shift from a funding system in which individuals were entitled to income support for residential care to one in which local authorities determined who obtained access to services by allocating a fixed budget, represented a fundamental change of approach. While it was widely recognized that there was scope for obtaining better value for money within existing budgets, there were also doubts about the adequacy of overall levels of funding in view of the increasing demands presented by an ageing population. In this respect, local authorities were faced with many of the same dilemmas as health authorities.

One of the risks that this gave rise to was that of cost shifting or buck passing. Put another way, faced with more needs than it was possible to accommodate within available resources, health authorities and local authorities might be tempted to transfer responsibility to each other. This risk was accentuated by the lack of clear definitions of health care on the one hand and community care on the other. In this situation, it was argued that health authorities and local authorities might adopt an increasingly narrow interpretation of their own responsibilities, leaving vulnerable clients and patients to fall between the two. These issues were highlighted in a report by the Ombudsman into the care of a patient in Leeds and the failure of the NHS to fund this care. In response, the Department of Health stated that continuing care was an integral part of the NHS. The Department also requested health authorities and local authorities to agree policies and eligibility criteria to ensure that services were in place to meet needs for long term health and social care. The purpose of this request was to avoid people in need not receiving the care they required. It followed that health authorities had to ensure adequate funding of NHS continuing care provision, including increasing expenditure on continuing care services where current levels of care were insufficient to enable the NHS to conform with local policies and eligibility criteria. At a time of considerable pressure on NHS and local authority budgets, it remains to be seen whether these measures will be sufficient to avoid a recurrence of the problems illustrated by the Leeds case.

In trying to avoid this, authorities in many parts of the country took the initiative to establish joint commissioning arrangements. These arrangements often built on earlier experience of joint planning and joint finance, and sought to ensure that there was a consistent approach between different agencies. In a number of places, there was interest not only in joint planning and needs assessment but also the pooling of resources for particular services or care groups. The development of joint commissioning suggested that in the longer term the division of responsibilities between the NHS and local government might be reviewed, with either local authorities taking responsibility for the commissioning of health services or the commissioning of social services passing to the NHS.

Conclusion

In this chapter, we have traced the development of the key elements in the NHS reforms in the period after 1991. We have shown how purchaser and provider roles were gradually separated with district health authorities taking on responsibility for purchasing and NHS trust status becoming the model of choice for provider units. An increasing number of GP practices entered the fundholding scheme while non-fundholding GPs were involved in purchasing through a variety of mechanisms. Contracts, or service agreements, provided the link between purchasers and providers and became increasingly sophisticated with time.

The question that arises from these developments is what was the impact on patients and service providers? Did the reforms achieve the improvements in services that were intended? Or was there an expansion of management costs, as the government's critics argued, with few if any benefits for patients? And what impact did competition have on the delivery of services? These are the questions addressed in the next chapter.

3 The Impact of the NHS Reforms

In an article for The Guardian in September 1992 I wrote:

> The NHS reforms are about to enter their third and most risky phase. This phase can be likened to the transition from childhood to adolescence. It follows a period of growth and development in which an infant that barely survived the trauma of premature birth has become steadily more mature and confident.
>
> Many of the difficulties encountered during childhood can be attributed to the abrupt and untimely way in which gestation was brought to an end. The midwife, Margaret Thatcher, insisted that the baby should be delivered within one year of conception. As a consequence, developments which should have occurred in the womb in practice took place in the first year of life.
>
> It was in this period, following publication of the white paper, *Working for Patients*, that the offspring began to take shape. Many of the features that were barely discernible at birth emerged more clearly and by the time the white paper had passed into law it was possible to see the nature of the being that had been created. At this point, in the summer of 1990, the second phase started.
>
> In this phase, there has been a period of sustained growth, and the baby has become a child. The child has acquired skills such as walking and talking and an identifiable personality of its own. It has even been known to disobey its parents on occasion. This has resulted in disciplinary action. The controls that are being imposed are so tight that the neighbours have sometimes wondered whether the child still lives at home.
>
> But with the election out of the way, and the autumn approaching, the infant prodigy has started to try out his newly acquired skills. This has resulted in demands for greater freedom and even a request to stay with friends

overnight. The current foster parents (the natural father has since moved to administer similar treatment to teachers and the police) are understandably anxious about these requests and are not yet sure that the child is sufficiently mature to be allowed this degree of latitude. At the same time, they realize that it won't be long before he leaves home for good. They know that independence in the longer term may be more easily achieved if risks are taken now.

It is these issues that the occupants of Richmond House agonize over. Having survived a difficult first year, and a sheltered childhood, should their offspring be given greater freedom? If he is, won't this result in mistakes which unsympathetic members of the family will blame on the parents? And wouldn't it be easier to protect the child from an increasingly hostile environment by maintaining its growth sheltered from the slings and arrows of fortune? These questions are as yet unresolved, but if the parents don't make up their minds soon the flowering adolescent may take matters into his own hands with unpredictable consequences for all.

To complicate the decision, in the same household there is an adopted child who has been told that she can leave home in April 1993. Like her sibling, she has suffered a series of setbacks, and was originally told she would be given her independence in 1991. But the adults thought it better to wait until her inheritance had been sorted out and for this reason there has been a delay. In the meantime, the two children have been encouraged to play together in the hope that they will become friends for life.

This metaphor may not exactly fit developments in the NHS (and its close relation, community care) but it highlights many of the dilemmas facing the current ministerial team. Above all, the metaphor illustrates that the key decision is whether to take some risks, knowing that mistakes will be made along the way, or to play safe, in the awareness that this strategy is also fraught with difficulties. It is a decision with which parents are familiar and which calls for careful judgment at a crucial stage in the life-cycle of change.

For Virginia Bottomley, a parent herself, the central choice is about the pace of development. Having taken over responsibility for the NHS and community care reforms from her predecessors, she is not in a position to question the direction of change. The most important decision at this stage is how quickly the reforms should proceed and the degree of freedom that should be allowed to local agencies in taking the reforms forward. In pondering this question, the Health Secretary is under pressure from her supporters to allow much greater competition in the internal health care market than has hitherto been permitted. She is also aware that many of those involved in running the NHS at a local level are keen to try out their new freedoms and functions and are increasingly impatient at the constraints imposed from above. And, to vary the metaphor, having let the genie out of the bottle, it will be difficult to squeeze it back in.

Nevertheless, Ministers are in a position to shape the framework within which competition occurs, not least by insisting that the market should be managed rather than left to the independent decisions of health authorities and NHS trusts. In this way it ought to be possible to relax some of the controls exercised by Ministers while ensuring that the process of change remains orderly. It is here that the role of regional health authorities is crucial. Ministers cannot direct the development of health services and community care from Whitehall and they must rely on an intermediate tier to act on their behalf.

Yet as things stand, the responsibilities of the intermediate tier are divided between regional health authorities and outposts of the NHS management executive in a bureaucratic confusion of the worst kind.

Faced with this confusion, Ministers need to act quickly. Above all, there must be the capacity at regional level to take a coherent view of the internal market and to manage competition in a way which balances greater freedom for health authorities and NHS trusts with an appropriate degree of regulation.

This is one of the issues that Mrs Bottomley has been considering over the summer, and an early decision is needed. If a single agency charged with managing the market is not established at the regional level, then the reforms could become discredited. The potential benefits in terms of greater efficiency and enhanced responsiveness to patients, which have already started to emerge, will not be realized.

The urgency of this issue is highlighted by the difficulties faced by hospitals in London which have had to cut back their services because they have not attracted sufficient contracts. Competition is already starting to have an impact, but there is no guarantee that market forces alone will produce an appropriate pattern of services.

The reality is that the market has to be regulated by a strategic body in a position to preserve the founding principles of the NHS at a time when new values are increasingly evident.

To return to the original metaphor, the adolescent may find himself in trouble if clear expectations are not established about the limits of independent action and standards of acceptable behaviour. If this were to happen, it would reflect badly not only on the offspring but also on the parents (Ham 1992d).

There are two points about this article which are central to an analysis of the impact of the NHS reforms. First, carrying out the reforms has involved a process of development in which their true nature has become clear only in the course of implementation. Second, at the heart of the reforms is the attempt to introduce a managed market in health care. A crucial judgement for Ministers is whether competition should be allowed to shape the future of the NHS, or whether the market should be managed to protect the interests of patients and the public. Each point will be considered in turn.

An Emergent Strategy

The reforms which stem from *Working for Patients* are quite unlike previous reorganizations of the NHS in that they are based on a document produced to a tight timetable and which bears all the hallmarks of a strategy only half thought through. There can be no starker contrast than with the 1974 reorganization which derived from a detailed blueprint developed by the Department of Health and Social Security and which, in design at least, left nothing to chance. In effect, managers and professionals have been discovering the importance of the separation of purchaser and provider roles, NHS trusts and GP fundholding and have been developing policy in the course of making the reforms work. Whether this is described as an emergent strategy or 'making it up as we go along', the effect is the same: much of the detail involved in the reforms was missing at their inception and policy has been made on the hoof.

The main benefit of this approach has been to allow those involved in purchasing and providing health services an unusual degree of freedom to influence and shape policy. To a significant extent, the real knowledge about the reforms and the way in which they are working rests with staff in the NHS rather than with civil servants in the Department of Health. This has been associated with a period of almost unprecedented innovation and experimentation in which NHS staff have used the freedoms available to them to test out what the reforms mean in practice. As a consequence, traditional relationships have been turned on their head with those at the centre struggling to keep pace with their colleagues on the ground.

The principal disadvantage of an emergent strategy has been a degree of ambiguity and inconsistency on the part of politicians responsible for the reforms. To oversimplify only a little, the Prime Ministers and Secretaries of State who have been associated with the reforms have each brought his or her agenda to the table (*see* Box 7). In the case of Margaret Thatcher, this was a belief in the value of the market as a means of improving performance. Kenneth Clarke shared this belief and in addition he was concerned to reform primary care through both GP fund-holding and the new contract for GPs introduced in 1990. William Waldegrave placed less emphasis on the market during his tenure as Secretary of State and instead gave priority to developing the role of health authorities as planners and purchasers. It was at this stage that the green paper on *The Health of the Nation* was published. Throughout this period Waldegrave stressed the contribution that health authorities could make to delivering the improvements in health set out in the green paper.

Box 7: Changing political priorities.

Margaret Thatcher	Competition and markets
Kenneth Clarke	The reform of primary care
William Waldegrave	*The Health of the Nation*
John Major	*The Patient's Charter*
Virginia Bottomley	Community care
Stephen Dorrell	Control of management costs

John Major, who took over as Prime Minister from Margaret Thatcher in November 1990, added a further layer of policy with the *Citizen's Charter* and its offspring, the *Patient's Charter*. These documents were an attempt to distinguish Majorism from Thatcherism and served to highlight those aspects of the NHS reforms concerned to improve the quality of services from the patient's perspective. For her part, Virginia Bottomley brought a particular interest in community care to the Department of Health and took a number of initiatives in this area, while continuing to oversee the implementation of policies initiated by her predecessors. To complete the process, Stephen Dorrell echoed Kenneth Clarke's concern to strengthen primary care while at the same time reiterating the government's commitment to the NHS. This was evident in the publication of two white papers on primary care in 1996 as well as a white paper on the future of the NHS as a whole. In addition, Dorrell emphasized the need to control management costs.

In these circumstances, it would have been surprising if the intentions of the architects of the reforms had not been diluted and to some extent distorted in the implementation process. It could be argued that civil servants provided the continuity that was lacking among politicians but in this respect too there were frequent changes in personnel at a senior level. In addition, there was not always a consistent view on the part of civil servants, particularly as the management executive endeavoured to strengthen its role and the policy divisions in the Department of Health came under challenge. On some issues, such as the Functions and Manpower Review conducted during 1993 (*see* below), former Secretaries of State were able to influence the direction of the reforms through Cabinet-level discussions, but for the most part it was left to the Secretary of State in office, advised by her officials, to determine the pattern of development. Given that *Working for Patients* itself was a broad framework rather than a detailed blueprint, it was to be expected that policy would be moulded on the basis not only of experience but also personal preferences and political judgement.

The other consequence of an emergent strategy was that difficulties arose during the course of implementation because insufficient thought had been given at the design stage to how the reforms would work in practice. In view of the inability to predict every contingency in advance, this was hardly surprising. Nevertheless, there were occasions when a little more forward planning might have prevented problems occurring. One obvious example concerned the process of setting budgets for GP fundholders. The inequity of a capitation formula for health authorities and an activity-based formula for fundholders quickly became apparent, and it was not easy to see how this could be rectified after the policy had been implemented.

Partly in anticipation of these kinds of problems, the management executive took a close interest in how the reforms were implemented. This first became evident during the course of 1990 when the Chief Executive and Deputy Chief Executive of the NHS indicated that the reforms should be taken forward in a planned and orderly fashion. This was variously described as a smooth take off, steady state and no surprises, but the intent was unambiguous: Ministers and officials wanted to ensure that the new market in health care was introduced slowly and with as little turbulence as possible. Put slightly differently, the aim was to manage the market in the initial stages in order to avoid harmful instability. As time went on, this emerged as a key theme within the reforms as a whole and one that was to test political judgement to its limits.

A Managed Market

The steady state policy was motivated by both political and managerial considerations. On the one hand, Ministers wanted to avoid the NHS reappearing in newspaper headlines in the run up to a general election. The prospect of hospitals finding themselves in financial difficulty as a result of the operation of the market was not attractive to the government and for this reason there was a strong political imperative to ensure that the reforms were implemented smoothly.

On the other hand, managers were aware of the huge programme of change involved in the reforms. Implementing this programme was made easier by the plan to phase in the reforms over a period of years but there was still a great deal to be done to put the basic building blocks in place from April 1991. Those on the inside of this process may one day publish their version of events, but from the outside there was a strong suggestion that both politicians and officials were having second thoughts and were on the verge of aborting take off altogether (Timmins, 1995).

In the event, this did not happen and implementation proceeded under the close eye of the NHS management executive. The *NHS and Community Care Bill* received the Royal Assent at the end of June 1990 paving the way for work to begin in earnest on detailed planning for April 1991. In anticipation of this, the NHS management executive requested health authorities to undertake a stock take of their plans for placing contracts. Health authorities were also advised to concentrate on block contracts to begin with to reduce the level of uncertainty and complexity for providers. In submitting reports to the management executive, health authorities were asked to identify large variations in how services were provided and how they planned to manage the risk of hospitals that depended heavily on income from extra contractual referrals (Ham, 1991).

The concerns of Ministers and civil servants were highlighted by a Department of Health memorandum on the likely effects of the reforms in London that was leaked to the Labour Party during 1990. The memorandum identified a strong possibility that health authorities outside London might decide to treat patients locally instead of referring them to teaching hospitals in London, partly because of the lower costs and spare capacity in the shire counties. The memorandum went on to record that GP fundholders might change their referrals in the same way. The effect would be to destabilize hospital provision in London leading to possible closures and cut backs.

The London memorandum was closely linked to the announcement in December 1990 of the allocation of resources to regional health authorities for 1991/92. Instead of redirecting cash on the weighted capitation basis set out in *Working for Patients*, Ministers gave more money than expected to the Thames regions. This provided a safety net to help authorities in London avoid bed closures and cut backs in the first year of the reforms. At the same time, additional resources were set aside to enable health authorities to clear underlying deficits in their budgets, thereby allowing all hospitals to compete from April 1991 on a comparable basis.

The NHS management executive continued to exercise detailed supervision of the operation of the reforms during 1991. The result was less a market in which a multitude of transactions took place between buyers and sellers than a command and control bureaucracy of the kind that has been dismantled across central and eastern Europe (Ham, 1992c). The central controls served their purpose by ensuring that the reforms were, on the whole, introduced in an orderly way. Despite well publicized problems at the Guy's and Lewisham and Bradford NHS trusts, which announced plans to make 900 staff redundant shortly after the market came into operation, most services continued to be provided in the same way during 1991/92.

It was, however, clear that it would be difficult to sustain this policy on a long term basis. The logic behind the reforms was that competition would act as a stimulus to improve performance, implying acceptance of a degree of instability as the market began to work. Furthermore, while Ministers may have been cautious about the pace of change, many of those working in the NHS were impatient to exercise the freedoms they believed they had been given. In recognition of this, the management executive announced that the second year of reforms would be a year of managed change in which the market would be allowed to come more fully into play.

In practice the impact of competition was felt most strongly in London and the major conurbations. This was in part because several hospitals in close proximity to each other created the conditions for a market to develop, and in part because of the way in which resources were allocated to district health authorities. The introduction of a weighted capitation formula at district level benefited health authorities in the shire counties at the expense of those in the inner cities. As a consequence, money moved away from the relatively expensive hospitals in the inner cities to those in surrounding areas with lower costs and greater accessibility. This was exactly what the Department of Health memorandum on London leaked to the Labour Party had predicted, and in October 1991 the government set up an inquiry into the future of health services in London led by Professor Sir Bernard Tomlinson.

At the time the inquiry was established, Ministers announced that four successful applications for NHS trust status in London would not go ahead until April 1993 to allow the recommendations of the Tomlinson inquiry to be taken into account. In this way, the signals thrown up by the market were joined with a strategic overview in an attempt to ensure an orderly process of change. Additional funds were also made available to the Thames regions to assist hospitals unable to attract sufficient contracts to balance their books. Outside London these issues were handled less through Tomlinson-style inquiries than by health authority purchasers working with each other and with providers to plan the reduction in hospital capacity that the market made inevitable. Whatever the preferred approach, the outcome was the same: the internal market became a managed market in which competition and planning went hand in hand.

The Tomlinson inquiry reported in October 1992 (*see* Box 8). In brief, it recommended the closure or merger of 10 inner London hospitals and the concentration of medical education and research on fewer sites. In parallel, proposals were put forward for strengthening primary care services at an estimated cost of £140 million. The *Tomlinson Report* provoked a storm of protest and criticism. With the exception of the plan to develop primary health care services, which received widespread support despite doubts about its feasibility, every aspect of Sir Bernard Tomlinson's analysis came under close scrutiny. Those institutions singled out for closure or major change of use mounted campaigns to oppose the inquiry's recommendations, and attention centred in particular on St Bartholomew's Hospital.

For its part, the government published a response to Tomlinson in February 1993, accepting most of the inquiry's analysis while acknowledging that some of the detailed proposals would need to be re-examined (Department of Health, 1993b). To assist in this process, further reviews were set up into the future of six specialist services and the quality of research in London. The Secretary of State also established the London Implementation Group, under the leadership of a former regional health authority chairman and general manager, to take responsibility for overseeing the process of change in London.

Box 8: The Tomlinson Report.

The *Tomlinson Report* recommended a shift of focus in London. This included increasing expenditure on primary care and community health services and reducing the number of hospitals and beds. The major changes affecting hospital services in the *Tomlinson Report* were:

- the redevelopment of University College Hospital (UCH) and the Middlesex on the UCH site

- the merger of St Bartholomew's and the Royal London hospitals on the Royal London site

- the merger of Guy's and St Thomas's on one site

- a rationalization of services in west London following the opening of the Westminster-Chelsea Hospital affecting the Charing Cross and Hammersmith hospitals among others

These changes were intended to rationalize the provision of specialist services on fewer sites and reduce the number of beds by between 2,000 and 7,000 by the end of the decade.

Source: *Tomlinson Report* (1992)

The unanswered question was whether change could be properly planned. On the one hand, health authorities were forcing the pace by moving contracts more rapidly than anticipated by Tomlinson and others. This became evident during 1993 when the Camden and Islington Health Authority announced its plans to move a number of services from University College Hospital (UCH) to other hospitals because of price differentials (Brindle, 1993a). On the other hand, GP fundholders did not always agree with the plans and priorities of health authorities and indicated their willingness to use their resources to frustrate these plans. This emerged as a key factor in south west London where Queen Mary's University Hospital in Roehampton was strongly supported by fundholders, even though a review undertaken by health authorities in the area identified it as the hospital most likely to close as services were rationalized from four sites to three (Brindle, 1993b).

The dilemma here for the government was that having deliberately moved away from old style, centralized planning to a more pluralistic set of arrangements, in which greater power was given to purchasers and providers at a local level, it became difficult to direct what happened in the NHS from the centre. In practice, Ministers did intervene in the market, not only to enforce a steady state in the first year but also to ensure that change was planned thereafter. As an example, the Camden and Islington Health Authority was instructed not to move contracts away from UCH in order that the rationalization of hospital services in that part of London went ahead as planned. In acting in this way Ministers were responding (whether consciously or not) to the concern expressed by Sir Bernard Tomlinson a year after publication of his report that the government had not intervened sufficiently in the market and that a more managed approach to change was needed.

Notwithstanding continuing criticism of the assumptions on which the Tomlinson report was based (Jarman, 1994), and acknowledgement even among advocates of change that a rethink was necessary (Maxwell, 1994), many of the proposals contained in the report were taken forward. In 1995 the government announced a series of decisions on the future of services in London, including the relocation of St Bartholomew's to the Royal London Hospital, the development of St Thomas's Hospital as a major specialist centre with Guy's Hospital concentrating on local hospital services, and changes in Margaret Thatcher's old constituency involving the development of Barnet General Hospital with Edgware Hospital taking on a reduced role. These developments proceeded in parallel with the merger of medical schools. And while the pill was sweetened with the promise of further investment in primary care and additional capital expenditure, the threat to both internationally renowned and local hospitals continued to cause controversy.

By intervening to determine the future of health care in London, Ministers were acknowledging the realities of a national health service in which ultimate responsibility for decisions rested with politicians in Westminster. Yet in so doing they ran the risk of weakening the competitive incentives designed to drive down costs and raise standards. While a managed market called for intervention on the part of Ministers and their officials, the danger this gave rise to was the creation of a culture in which providers who were failing came to expect that they would receive political protection and extra funding. Striking the right balance between management and the market was crucial to the success of the reforms and yet, as part of the emergent strategy, it was an issue whose significance was only recognized during the course of implementation.

In practice, it was not until 1993, when Ministers set in hand a series of reviews to define the functions to be performed in the NHS in future, that regulating and managing the market was even acknowledged to be a key issue. In the absence of a clear lead from the centre, it was left to local purchasers and providers to work out their best way forward, often with the support and assistance of regional health authorities and management executive outposts. This resulted in major reviews of the future of hospital and health services in areas such as Birmingham, Bristol, West Yorkshire and Newcastle.

National guidance on market regulation was eventually published at the end of 1994 in a document entitled *The Operation of the NHS Internal Market: local freedoms, national responsibilities*. This set out rules governing purchaser mergers, provider mergers, dealing with providers in difficulty, and collusive behaviour. In the event the guidance was something of a damp squib, its publication coming too late to have a significant bearing on the service changes already taking place.

The Impact on Patients

In analysing the impact of the reforms, it is as well to remember the title of the white paper from which they derive. *Working for Patients* may have been a response to financial and managerial problems in the NHS but its ostensible purpose was to improve services to patients. Fascinating as innovations such as GP fund-holding and NHS trusts may be, the ultimate test of the reforms is what difference they have made for patients. This is the yard-stick against which the success or failure of the reforms should be judged and it is here that the debate continues between the government and its critics.

When Ministers assess the impact of the reforms on patients, they emphasize two factors above all others. First, they claim that more patients are being treated than ever before, citing increases in hospital activity levels in support of this view. Second, Ministers maintain that there have been improvements in waiting times, especially for those patients waiting a long time for an operation. This is usually attributed to the *Patient's Charter* which, when it was published in 1991, promised that no patients should wait longer than two years for surgery. Indeed, the *Patient's Charter* and the publication of performance tables based on the standards contained within it are credited with a range of improvements in services to patients. Beyond these specific claims, Ministers also contend that there has been an overall improvement in quality as NHS trusts have responded to the challenge of the market to raise standards of care. In this case, examples such as improved access to services and initiatives to enhance patient convenience are invoked to illustrate the impact of the reforms.

While there is an element of truth in all of these claims, they need to be treated with caution. To begin with, the increase in the number of patients treated is arguably the result of the additional funding provided for the NHS in recent years rather than the reforms *per se* (Bloor and Maynard, 1993). The rate of growth in NHS spending was significantly greater in the period 1990-93 than during the 1980s and this undoubtedly enabled more patients to be treated (*see* Table 1). There is also anecdotal evidence to suggest that providers have improved their systems for counting and recording the work done. Some of the increase in activity that has occurred is almost certainly an artefact of better information systems rather than a reflection of genuine productivity gains. A further factor to bear in mind is that there was a change in the way in which patient activity in hospitals was classified and this led some analysts to argue that the increases cited by government spokesmen were artificially inflated (Radical Statistics Health Group, 1992 and 1995).

The reduction in waiting times should be viewed in a similar light. The longest waiting times have indeed fallen and no patient now has to wait longer than two years for an operation. There has also been a reduction in the number of patients waiting between one and two years. To some extent, however, these improvements have been achieved at the expense of an increase in the number of patients waiting for less than a year. Equally significant is the fact that the reduction in waiting times has been brought about less by the market than through earmarked funding and direct political intervention. Ministers have made it clear that the jobs of health authority chairmen and general managers who fail to deliver the government's targets are on the line, and it is this that has served as a spur to improved performance.

As far as overall improvements in quality are concerned, it is difficult to sustain the argument that the reforms have been responsible for any dramatic change of policy or practice. Raising the standard of health care has been an issue high on the health policy agenda right through the 1980s and was emphasized particularly in the *Griffiths Report* of 1983. As a consequence, there have been many improvements in service provision and a stronger focus on the patient's perspective. The nature of the changes that have occurred has been demonstrated in a series of reports and studies. The NHS reforms may have helped to continue what was already happening and given fresh impetus to existing initiatives but they did not in any sense represent a radical departure from previous policies to improve quality (Jones, Lester and West, 1994).

Other evidence is equally inconclusive. Taking the *Patient's Charter* first, the publication of performance tables setting out the record of NHS trusts in achieving the standards set by the government has made more transparent variations in performance and has acted as a spur for poorly performing trusts to focus on the quality of their services. Although the absence of independent validation means that caution is needed in interpreting the results, data included in the performance tables suggest that standards have risen over time, for example in improving access to treatment. Against this, a report by the Ombudsman published in 1994 was critical of the record of the NHS in responding to patient complaints and argued that the more fragmented structure introduced as a consequence of the reforms had made it difficult to co-ordinate the provision of care. On the other hand, in the same year, the British Social Attitudes' Survey reported that levels of dissatisfaction with the NHS had fallen, suggesting that the reforms might be at last bringing benefits for some patients.

The Shift in the Balance of Power

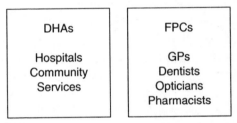

Figure 5: The old NHS.

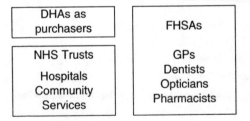

Figure 6: The purchaser/provider split.

The most important effect of the reforms, even if unanticipated, was the shift in the balance of power within the NHS (Ham,

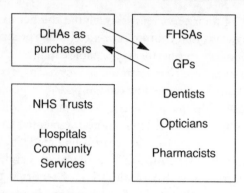

Figure 7: DHAs form alliances with GPs and FHSAs.

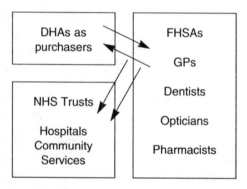

Figure 8: DHA/FHSA/GP alliances put pressure on providers.

1993a; Klein, 1995a). This is illustrated in Figures 5–8. The figures show the changing nature of relationships as the reforms unfolded, demonstrating how in the old NHS district health authorities and the former family practitioner committees (FPCs) rarely came into contact. The separation of purchaser and provider roles in district health authorities (Figure 6) led these authorities to open up a dialogue with family health services authorities and GPs (Figure 7). The developing alliance between district health authorities, family health services authorities and GPs has put pressure on NHS trusts to improve their performance (Figure 8). As a consequence power has shifted from purchasers to providers, from hospital specialists to GPs, and to some degree from doctors to managers. The old system of planning by decibels, in which the providers of acute services won the biggest share of resources, has been brought into question, and there has been a shift of emphasis in favour of public health.

In relation to public health, *The Health of the Nation* strategy provided a framework within which health authorities in England have been working to improve the health of their populations. At a national level, a Cabinet committee was established to oversee the implementation of the strategy and to promote co-ordination between government departments. Figures produced by the Department of Health suggested that good progress was being made towards most of the targets set out in *The Health of the Nation*, and in 1996 it was suggested that the environment should be added as a further key area in the national health strategy. Despite this progress, a review by the National Audit Office recommended that the Department of Health review the programme, revisiting and raising targets where progress was good, taking action to improve performance where progress was poor, and improving the quality and availability of data to support monitoring.

In the case of primary care, GPs occupy a pivotal position in the new NHS with resources and services moving increasingly in the direction of primary care. This was explicitly acknowledged in October 1994 when the government published its plans on the future of purchasing. At the heart of these plans was a concern to develop a primary care led NHS through the integration of district health authorities and family health services authorities and the expansion of GP fundholding. Subsequently, Ministers launched a debate on the future of primary care. This took the form of a listening exercise led by Gerald Malone, the Minister of State for Health, and it resulted in a series of proposals for strengthening primary care and offering GPs a wider range of contractual options. Legislation to give effect to these proposals was published at the end of 1996 (*see* chapter 4).

Four examples illustrate the move towards a primary care led NHS. First, there is increasing emphasis on the development of shared care between GPs and specialists in areas such as asthma and diabetes. Second, specialists in some districts are holding their out-patient clinics in GPs' surgeries rather than in hospitals. This often involves 'treat and teach' arrangements in which GPs develop their own skills by sitting in on the consultation. Third, many practices are carrying out a wider range of diagnostic tests in their surgeries, thereby reducing demands on hospitals. And fourth, GPs are employing additional staff in primary care teams to enable them to deliver more services to patients, for example, physiotherapists, chiropodists, dietitians and counsellors.

Taken together, these developments are profoundly altering the shape of the NHS. In organizational terms, the old hierarchical, integrated structures have been replaced by a more diverse (some would say fragmented) set of contractual arrangements. Within these arrangements, established relationships have come into question. The stronger focus on primary care developed by GPs, health authorities and fundholders has been matched by rapid changes in relation to secondary care and considerable uncertainty as to the future pattern of hospital services. Hospital managers and professionals have found their own position under increasing challenge as those involved in primary care have come to exert greater influence.

Nowhere is this better illustrated than in relation to GP fundholding. With the purchasing power to back their decisions, fundholders are in a strong position to negotiate improvements in services on behalf of their patients. This they have done in a range of ways, including offering additional services in their practices, cutting waiting times for out-patient appointments and elective surgery, and improving communication with hospital doctors and managers. Ministers have used these changes in support of the argument that the reforms really are working for patients. Against this, critics maintain that fundholding has undermined equity within the NHS, and that the costs of the scheme outweigh the benefits.

As we noted in chapter 2, the evidence on fundholding does not point in a consistent direction. Furthermore, what evidence there is is often limited to a small number of practices with inadequate controls to enable rigorous comparisons to be made between fundholding and non-fundholding practices. Recognizing these limitations, research into fundholding in its early phases suggested that there were few differences between fundholding and non-fundholding practices in the way in which they provided care. Later studies painted a more complex picture with a number of researchers claiming that fundholders had brought about changes in services for patients. The most powerful support for fundholding came from Glennerster and his colleagues (1992 and 1994) who argued that fundholders had proved more effective purchasers than health authorities.

Notwithstanding these claims, other researchers remained sceptical. Coulter, for example, following a review of the evidence, concluded that:

'We simply do not know enough about the risks and benefits of the alternative models of health care purchasing . . . Claims that GP fundholding has proved to be a success are premature. Yet again policy is being formulated without waiting for adequate evidence' (Coulter, 1995, p238).

Similarly, Petchey (1995) urged caution in interpreting the evidence on fundholding, noting that the achievements of fundholders might in part be a consequence of their status as innovators rather than being attributable to fundholding *per se*. For their part, Dixon and Glennerster summarized their review of the literature by noting:

'The financial incentives of fundholding seem to be curbing the upward trend in prescribing costs, but the effect on rates of referral to hospital is unclear. Fundholders are challenging the traditional interface of primary and secondary care and offering more services in house. Significant improvements in access to and the process of care have been secured by some fundholders. Giving budgets to general practitioners has been associated with a noticeable change in their relationship with hospital consultants.

Set against these important gains, some drawbacks are evident. The costs to the NHS of contracting with many fundholding practices are unknown but estimated to be high. While fundholders report greater access to care, there is a weight of anecdotal (though not yet hard) evidence that a two tier service is operating. Research suggests that fundholders have been funded more generously than non-fundholding practices' (Dixon and Glennerster, 1995, p729).

The most comprehensive assessment of fundholding, that carried out by the Audit Commission, was published in 1996. In a wide ranging review, the Audit Commission noted that most fundholders had achieved some improvements for their patients, most notably improved communications with hospitals and more cost-effective prescribing. However, only the best managed practices had had a major impact on services. Overall, the costs of fundholding outweighed the efficiency savings achieved, and the Audit Commission made a series of proposals designed to strengthen the scheme and ensure its benefits were extended to other practices. These proposals included improving management skills and capacity within primary care and developing the role of health authorities in support of fundholders (Audit Commission, 1996).

The argument was further complicated by reports suggesting that many of the changes brought about by fundholders had also been achieved by health authorities working with GPs through locality commissioning arrangements and GP commissioning groups (Black, Birchall and Trimble, 1994; Graffy and Williams, 1994) and by the development of hybrid approaches combining features of fundholding and health authority purchasing. This was evident both in the development of total purchasing projects and multifunds linking together GPs in a number of practices, and in the establishment of joint working between health authorities and GPs. Convergence in purchasing was driven by the fact that neither health authority purchasing nor fundholding was by itself sufficient to achieve sustained benefits for patients.

Experience suggested that challenge was to combine the most positive features of each, namely the sensitivity to patients of GPs and the ability of health authorities to plan for whole communities and to take a strategic view (Ham, 1996a). As GPs took on greater responsibility for budgets with the expansion of fundholding, health authorities were able to concentrate on their strategic tasks and to hold GPs to account for the use of resources through the accountability framework for fundholders (*see* Box 9). To this extent, the debate about the merits or otherwise of fundholding gave way to a discussion of how GPs and health authorities could best work together. As this happened, the key challenge was how to ensure consistency and equity between different purchasers without this stifling initiative and while keeping transaction costs within acceptable limits.

Managing the New NHS

The concern over management costs was not confined to fundholding. During the course of 1993, through a series of Parliamentary questions, Alan Milburn, a backbench Labour MP, extracted information from the Department of Health on the increase in the number of managers that had resulted from the reforms. This illustrated that in the UK the number of managers rose from 6,091 in 1989/90 to 20,478 in 1992/93. Over the same period the number of administrative and clerical staff rose from 144,582 to 166,363. There was a much smaller increase in the numbers of other staff employed in the NHS.

While some of the increase in management costs could be explained by a reclassification of nursing staff into management grades, there was also a real growth in the number of managers employed as a direct result of government policies. Part of this cost increase arose from the 1983 Griffiths' reforms and the

Box 9: An accountability framework for fundholding.

Management accountability

☐ preparation of annual practice plan;

☐ signalling major shifts in purchasing intentions;

☐ preparation of an annual performance report;

☐ review performance with the health authority within the national framework.

Accountability to patients and the wider public

☐ publishing information, e.g. annual practice plan and performance report;

☐ involving patients in service planning;

☐ ensuring an effective complaints system.

Financial accountability

☐ preparation of annual accounts for independent audit;

☐ providing monthly information for monitoring by the health authority;

☐ securing agreement to proposed use of savings for material or equipment purchases (including those relating to health education), improvement of premises, clinical audit, research and training;

☐ stating planned contribution to the local efficiency targets set by the NHS executive.

Clinical and professional accountability

☐ participating in clinical audit of GMS activities;

☐ ensuring that agreed audit programmes are completed by hospital and community health care service providers.

---

remainder was due to the extra workload following *Working for Patients*. It became clear that the shift from an integrated to a contract system involved additional transaction costs associated with negotiating and monitoring contracts and related billing and invoicing arrangements. What was difficult to judge was whether the expenditure on management had produced commensurate benefits in terms of gains in efficiency and improvements in quality.

Prompted by concerns about the increase in management costs, the Secretary of State for Wales, John Redwood, placed a moratorium on new management posts in Wales and issued guidance asking health authorities and trusts to reduce the percentage of their budgets spent on management. In a thinly veiled attack on the policies of his predecessors, Redwood criticized the number of 'men in grey suits' in the NHS and called for a reduction in bureaucracy to enable more money to be spent on direct patient care. As this debate developed, the Functions and Manpower Review, initiated by Virginia Bottomley, was examining how the structure of the NHS should be changed to bring it into line with the objectives of the reforms.

The Functions and Manpower Review grew out of an analysis of the intermediate tier of management begun in 1992 (Ham, 1993b). This analysis focused particularly on the respective roles of regional health authorities and management executive outposts, and their relationship with purchasers and providers. At the beginning of 1993 the Secretary of State announced that regional health authorities had been asked to reduce the number of staff they employed to a maximum of 200 each. At the same time, she established the Functions and Manpower Review under the leadership of Kate Jenkins, from the NHS Policy Board, and Alan Langlands, then Deputy Chief Executive of the NHS.

The terms of reference eventually agreed for the Review were wide ranging, encompassing not only the role of the inter-mediate tier but also the work of the Department of Health as well as management arrangements at a local level. The Jenkins/ Langlands Review reported to the Secretary of State in July 1993 setting out various options for consideration. The government's decisions on these options were announced in October 1993 in a report entitled *Managing the New NHS* (Ham, 1993c). These decisions centred on three key elements: the merger of district health authorities and family health services authorities; the abolition of regional health authorities; and a streamlined NHS management executive operating through eight regional offices.

Cutting across all these elements was a policy of reducing management costs.

In one sense, these proposals were a tidying up exercise designed to reduce duplication and clarify management arrangements. This was behind the decision to abolish regional health authorities and to merge district health authorities and family health services authorities. Similarly, the changes to the management executive were intended to reduce central intervention in the NHS and establish the management executive clearly as the head office of the NHS within the Department of Health. The creation of regional offices of the management executive meant that for the first time there would be a single agency at the regional level in a position to relate to both purchasers and providers. It also opened up the possibility that regional offices, acting as part of the civil service rather than the NHS, would strengthen rather than weaken central control of health services.

The fact that a regional structure has been retained at all, when some were arguing for its complete abolition, suggests that Ministers recognize the dangers of unrestricted competition and are committed to regulating the operation of the market. *Managing the New NHS* was similar to *Working for Patients* in that it indicated the overall direction of the government's thinking without the supporting detail. Accordingly, 12 functions' analysis groups were established to supply this detail. These groups focused on the eight key areas identified in *Managing the New NHS* (*see* Figure 9). The reports of these groups were published in 1994 together with the Banks Review of the wider Department of Health and a report on the organization of public health in England. As a result of these reports, the Department of Health was streamlined and restructured around its main responsibilities of public health, health care and social care; the NHS management executive, restyled as the NHS executive, was given responsibility for the central management of the NHS through its headquarters and regional offices; and further reductions in the number of staff in both the NHS executive and the rest of the Department were announced.

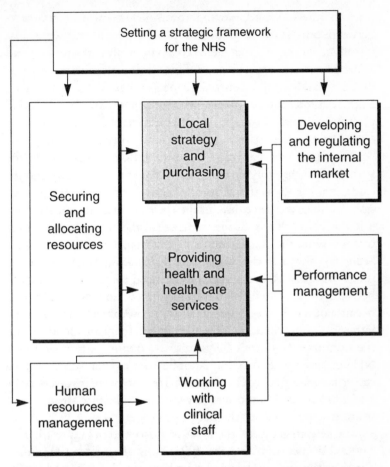

Figure 9: Functions carried out by the NHS (Source: Department of Health (1993c)).

Legislation to abolish regional health authorities and to integrate district health authorities and family health services authorities was published later in the year and at the same time an efficiency scrutiny was set up with the aim of reducing paperwork in the NHS. The latter reported in May 1996 and made a series of recommendations designed to produce savings of £40 million, including simplifying the system of extra contractual referrals and moving towards longer term contracts between purchasers and providers. Tight controls were also introduced over management costs in health authorites and NHS trusts with targets being set by Ministers for cutting expenditure and releasing resources for patient care. GP fundholders, as the cornerstone of the government's policy to improve NHS performance, were exempt from these controls.

Taken together, these decisions amounted to nothing less than a further reorganization of the NHS, perhaps not on the scale of *Working for Patients*, but in some ways equally significant. Echoing the starting point of this chapter, this reorganization was necessary because, in the spirit of an emergent strategy, it had become clear that the structure of the NHS was no longer in tune with the requirements of the reforms. In this case, a Secretary of State who was intuitively unsympathetic to structural change was persuaded of the need to take action, both because of the logic of developments within the NHS and because of wider developments within government. As far as the latter was concerned, the pressures on government spending and the need to search for savings at every opportunity meant that NHS management costs could not be exempt from scrutiny. Both the Prime Minister's Office and the Treasury were involved in the Functions and Manpower Review and pressure from these sources helped to force the pace of change.

The new structure of the NHS is illustrated in Figure 10. This came into operation in April 1996. From that date, 100 unified health authorities replaced district health authorities and family health services authorities, and the NHS executive's regional offices took over the functions of regional health authorities. In parallel, fundholding entered a new phase with around 50 total purchasing projects going live. NHS trusts were also affected by organizational change as proposals were put forward in some parts of the country to rationalize the configuration of trusts through mergers.

In the new structure, health authorities were identified as having the following roles:

strategy: agreeing with GPs, local people and agencies what needs to be done to ensure that national and local priorities are met through general practitioner led purchasing;

monitoring: advising on budget allocations to fund-holders and ensuring that the way in which general practitioners fulfil their purchasing role is in the interests of patients and secures value for money;

support: assisting practices to become fundholders and involving all practices in wider purchasing deci-

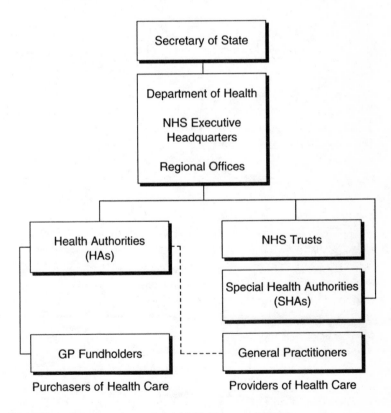

Figure 10: New structure of the NHS (Source: NHSE).

sions, as well as supporting the development of primary care through advice, investment and training.

With the abolition of regional health authorities, the new health authorities have a major responsibility as the only statutory bodies at a local level in a position to oversee the health of the population and the development of services. This is illustrated in Figure 11 which shows how health authorities hold the ring in the NHS and are at the heart of the local health system. The drive towards a primary care led NHS has placed their partners in primary care inside the ring. While the role of health authorities in direct commissioning may be diminishing, their other responsibilities are growing in importance. This includes holding GPs to account for the use of resources, liaising with local authorities and other agencies in the joint development of

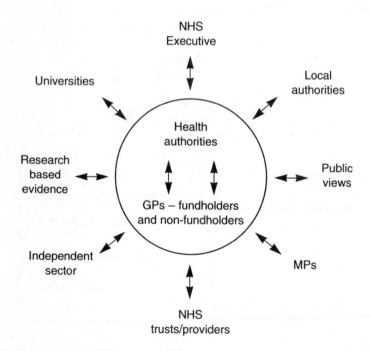

Figure 11: Relationships in the NHS.

services and in improving the health of the population, and engaging the public in a dialogue on the future of health and health services.

An Assessment

Independent studies of the impact of the reforms highlight the difficulty for researchers in evaluating the effects of the changes that have taken place. In the most comprehensive early assessment, Robinson and Le Grand (1994) detected relatively few changes in the first stages of implementation. Notwithstanding this, Le Grand suggested, on the basis of the work that had been done, that there were grounds for believing that the reforms were beginning to have a positive effect (Le Grand, 1994). Equally, he noted the challenge of making an assessment on the basis of limited evidence and in the absence of systematic research. A further confounding factor, as noted earlier, was the increase in expenditure on the NHS during this period and the difficulty of disentangling the impact of the reforms from that of other changes occurring at the same time.

A more upbeat assessment was made by the Organisation for Economic Cooperation and Development (OECD, 1994). In an analysis widely cited by health ministers in support of the reforms, the OECD found much to commend in the changes that had been introduced, highlighting fundholding in particular as an example of success, and pointing to 'encouraging' early results from the performance of NHS trusts (OECD, 1994, p76). These conclusions were challenged by Bloor and Maynard (1994) who pointed to the inadequacies of the evidence on which they were based. In a separate review, Maynard and Bloor (1996) concluded that:

'The success of the NHS reforms has been mixed' (p607).

This is also the view of Klein who notes evidence of increasing activity and declining waiting lists while drawing attention to the failure of the reforms to increase patient choice and to make staff more satisfied (Klein, 1995a). My own assessment reached the following conclusion:

> 'any efficiency gains resulting from the reforms have been achieved at the expense of equity losses . . . Less tangibly, the reforms have introduced a new dynamic into the management of health services. This has resulted in a shift in the balance of power and a greater capacity for addressing weaknesses in service delivery.
>
> Set against these gains, the separation of purchaser and provider responsibilities has led to an increase in management costs . . . What remains open to dispute is whether the benefits outweigh the additional costs that have been incurred' (Ham, 1996b, pp21–3).

These evaluations suggest that market-oriented reforms are no more a panacea than reforms based on planning and regulation. If there are no quick fix solutions to the problems faced by health policy makers, then there is a need for caution in exploring radical alternatives. And indeed, this is precisely what is happening with the government setting out a programme of change in its white paper on the future of the NHS which owes little to ideology and everything to pragmatism (Secretary of State for Health, 1996a). This indicates that politicians have embraced a new realism, recognizing the intractability of the problems confronting health services and the need to make progress one step at a time (Ham, 1996c). If this is the case, then what lessons can be drawn from experience of implementing the NHS reforms in the period since 1991?

The main lessons are summarized in Box 10 which outlines some principles which I have suggested should guide policy towards the NHS in the future. These principles are based on the view that there is value in maintaining a separation between purchaser and provider roles. This should be used as a way of ensuring accountability for the use of resources rather than as a means of promoting competition. Relationships between purchasers and providers would be based on collaboration and long term commitments. However, contestability would act as a spur to efficiency and responsiveness and would enable purchasers to bring about improvements in performance by moving services between providers if other approaches failed. As such contestability would offer a middle way between a planned approach and a health care market.

Box 10: Lessons from the NHS reforms.

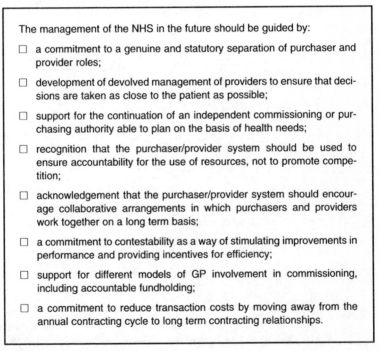

The management of the NHS in the future should be guided by:

☐ a commitment to a genuine and statutory separation of purchaser and provider roles;

☐ development of devolved management of providers to ensure that decisions are taken as close to the patient as possible;

☐ support for the continuation of an independent commissioning or purchasing authority able to plan on the basis of health needs;

☐ recognition that the purchaser/provider system should be used to ensure accountability for the use of resources, not to promote competition;

☐ acknowledgement that the purchaser/provider system should encourage collaborative arrangements in which purchasers and providers work together on a long term basis;

☐ a commitment to contestability as a way of stimulating improvements in performance and providing incentives for efficiency;

☐ support for different models of GP involvement in commissioning, including accountable fundholding;

☐ a commitment to reduce transaction costs by moving away from the annual contracting cycle to long term contracting relationships.

Source: Ham (1996b)

Conclusion

In this chapter, we have analysed the impact of the reforms in the first six years of operation. In so doing we have highlighted the evolutionary nature of the reforms and the increasing under-standing that has been gained of their impact during the process of implementation. It has become clear that a delicate balance has to be struck between management and competition and Ministers have demonstrated their willingness to intervene in the market when required so to do.

The most important effect of the reforms to date has been to change the balance of power within the NHS. This has made providers more accountable to purchasers and it has strength-ened the position of primary care. GP fundholding has been at the forefront of these developments, although doubts remain about the long term viability of the fundholding scheme. As a consequence of these changes, there has been a fundamental shift in views and attitudes within the NHS and an ability to tackle problems that previously appeared intractable.

One of the concerns that has emerged is the increase in man-agement costs that has resulted from the reforms. This applies throughout the NHS and was a key factor behind the Functions and Manpower Review conducted during 1993. As a result of the Review, the NHS has been reorganized and a new streamlined structure put in place. This has helped in reducing management costs and continuing action on this issue can be anticipated.

The impact of the reforms on patients is more difficult to assess. The claims made by Ministers of increases in the number of patients treated and reductions in waiting times need to be treated cautiously. Insofar as there have been improvements in these areas, they are probably the consequence of increased levels of funding for the NHS in the period since 1990 rather than the reforms alone. More positively, patients in some parts of the NHS have benefited from the changes to primary care that have occurred, although there are continuing concerns about morale in general practice. The challenge now is to build on the most positive elements of the reforms in the more pragmatic spirit which has entered the health policy debate.

4   The Future of the Reforms

The changes to the structure of the NHS introduced in 1996 in effect completed the organizational transformation begun in 1991. As a consequence of these changes, the NHS in England is made up of:

- over 400 NHS trusts responsible for managing hospital and community health services;

- 100 health authorities responsible for commissioning health services for the communities they serve;

- general practice fundholders (involving 13,400 GPs in 1996) who are responsible for purchasing services for over 50 per cent of the population.

It would, however, be wrong to conclude that the introduction of these organizational changes means that the reforms themselves have been implemented in full. Notwithstanding the prospect of greater organizational stability following the creation of the new health authorities and the changes at the regional level, the NHS continues to resemble a service in a state of permanent revolution with fundholding and GP commissioning evolving rapidly in different directions and with a major new agenda concerned with the future of primary care.

Furthermore, given the emergent nature of the strategy on which the reforms are based, and the fact that the ultimate destination has never been specified by politicians and their advisers, it would in any case be difficult to know when the end point had been reached even assuming this were to happen. Indeed, the reforms contain within their design a number of self-correcting mechanisms enabling the direction of travel to be adjusted during the course of implementation (Ham, 1996a; Klein, 1995a). As a consequence, political ideology has been mediated by managerial pragmatism and an assessment of what is likely to be acceptable to the health care professions. Nowhere is this more apparent than in relation to markets and competition, the core ideas at the heart of the reforms. The policy message articulated by politicians changed significantly between 1989 and 1996 and by the end of that period a new agenda had come to emerge out of the old.

The End of Competition?

To outside observers, as well as to those responsible for implementing the reforms, it was striking how the radical aspirations of the pro-market reformers who initiated the reforms quickly gave way to a more sober appreciation of the limited scope for competition in many parts of the NHS and the need for purchasers and providers to work together to achieve benefits for patients. The cat was let out of the bag by William Waldegrave when he was the Secretary of State for Health. In an interview, he explained that the NHS market:

> 'isn't a market in the real sense . . . it's competition in the sense that there will be comparative information available. It's not a market in that people don't go bust and make profits and all that, but it's using market-like mechanisms to provide better information' (Smith, 1991, p712).

Waldegrave's comments were echoed in a major speech given by Virginia Bottomley at the Royal Society of Medicine in 1995 shortly before she was moved from the post of Secretary of State for Health. Reviewing the development of the reforms, Bottomley noted that:

> 'Hospitals are kept on their toes by the power of health authorities and fundholders to demand improvements in quality, in service and in the effectiveness with which they use resources.'

She continued:

> 'Competition *by comparison* is made possible by the vast strides we have made in recent years in the availability of clinical, financial and outcome information'(emphasis added).

Building on these themes, the Secretary of State went on to argue for a:

'. . . long-term and strategic view. A great deal can and will be achieved through the purchaser/provider system. As that relationship matures, I want to see purchasing become more sophisticated. I want to see greater use of longer-term contracts between health authorities, fundholders and NHS Trusts . . . The new NHS requires a strategic oversight . . . There are many issues . . . where it is important to take a broad view. The implementation of our strategy for developing cancer services is just one example of where we shall achieve a long-term goal by working together within the framework offered by the new NHS' (Bottomley, 1995, p7).

Bottomley's successor, Stephen Dorrell, also played down the role of markets in health care and focused instead on using the management reforms (sic) to increase efficiency and raise standards (Ham, 1996d). At the same time, Dorrell endorsed the need for collaboration between purchasers and providers and long term relationships. The importance of the latter was reinforced by the drive to reduce management costs. As the efficiency scrutiny into NHS paperwork noted in its 1996 report, cutting back on unnecessary bureaucracy hinged crucially on simplifying contracting arrangements and moving away from the annual contracting cycle. This in turn implied a more limited role for markets, at least compared with what had been expected at the time the reforms were announced, and a stronger emphasis on planning and collaboration.

Yet if competition and markets were words that rarely crossed the lips of politicians, they were certainly part of the vocabulary of the NHS at a local level. Despite the reluctance of Health Ministers to advocate competition as a strategy of reform, both health authorities and fundholders in some parts of the country were prepared to exercise their purchasing power to bring about improvements in services for patients. An example arose in East Anglia in 1996 when the health authorities in Suffolk and East Norfolk announced their intention of moving contracts from a poorly performing provider. The effect was to undermine the viability of the NHS trust concerned, leading to what the media represented as the first trust to go bankrupt. Elsewhere, fundholders were not slow to switch contracts if they perceived benefits for patients, although the effect was usually less dramatic given that fundholders controlled a smaller proportion of the overall budget. Similarly, health authorities facing the prospect of financial deficits explored ways of saving money, for example by repatriating services and contracts from distant providers to ones that were local. To the extent that competition was alive and well locally, and in practice this varied a great deal between areas, there was a dissonance between the policy message at the centre and what was actually happening in practice.

Virginia Bottomley's arguments for a long term and strategic view were in part a response to criticism about the lack of a vision at the centre. Commenting on these issues in an editorial for the *British Medical Journal* in 1994, I wrote:

> 'As things stand, there is no coherent strategy guiding the development of the NHS and there is a suspicion that the current occupants of Richmond House are not much interested in developing one. Tactics have come to dominate strategy, and ministers have seemed more concerned with keeping the NHS out of the headlines than with articulating a clear vision for the future . . . The reality is that short term political horizons dominate the thinking of politicians and militate against debate on matters of more fundamental importance. This has left a vacuum that civil servants, themselves preoccupied with organisational changes and steering implementation of the NHS reforms, have shown no inclination to fill' (Ham, 1994, p351).

Subsequently, some progress was made in clarifying the policy framework and in ensuring greater coherence in the guidance on priorities issued annually to health authorities. As part of this process, Ministers identified the main government policies as *The Health of the Nation, Caring for People, The Patient's Charter* and *A Primary Care Led NHS*. Work on strategy was taken further in 1996 when the government published a white paper on the future of the NHS (Secretary of State for Health, 1996a). The white paper came down firmly against further structural change, focusing instead on restating the government's commitment to the NHS and setting out the principles intended to guide the NHS into the future. A number of strategic objectives were identified in the white paper. These were to create a well informed public, a seamless service, decision making based on the latest clinical evidence, a highly trained and skilled workforce, and a service that responds to patients' needs. In effect, the white paper signalled an end to big bang reform and a concentration instead on pragmatic problem solving (Ham, 1996c). In so doing, it placed a further nail in the coffin of markets.

With competition increasingly out of favour among politicians, a new policy agenda has begun to emerge (Ham, 1996d). This owes less to a belief in market forces than a desire to use the organizational changes brought about by the NHS reforms to achieve other objectives. Delivery of the current agenda hinges on effective planning and coordination but has been made more salient by the separation of purchaser and provider roles on which the reforms are based. Not least, the existence of health authorities able to take an independent view of the population's health needs without being beholden to particular providers has changed the way in which decisions are made. Among other things, as we noted in earlier chapters, it has resulted in a shift of emphasis towards primary care, a focus on health as well as health services, and a concern to use the contracting system to improve access and patient convenience. In addition, through the research and development programme, health authorities and fundholders have received a wide range of advice and support on clinical effectiveness, the intention being that they should use this advice in deciding what services to purchase and where to place contracts (*see* below). None of these policies was in place at the time *Working for Patients* was published but all have risen to prominence on the back of the reforms. The policy on primary care is of particular significance currently and we now turn to a consideration of developments in this area.

Primary Care

During 1996, the policy of developing a primary care led NHS received increasing attention. The phrase 'a primary care led NHS' was used originally as part of a policy statement made in 1994 on the development of purchasing and the expansion of fundholding. As time went on, it came to be used more widely to refer not only to fundholding but also to the involvement of non-fundholding GPs in commissioning and to the provision of services in primary care. In discussing a primary care led NHS, Ministers emphasized the need for decisions to be taken as close to patients as possible, for GPs to be the coordinators of care, and for there to be effective team working between the different professionals providing this care.

As the debate developed attention focused on ways in which the traditional strengths of general practice could be developed as well as options for tackling problems of morale and recruitment in general practice. The latter had complex causes including the administrative burden of the 1990 GP contract, workload pressures, and rising patient demands and expectations. Notwithstanding the additional influence gained by GPs as a consequence of the NHS reforms, there was evidence that general practice was losing its attractions both to qualified doctors and those in training. The paradox of general practice was one of the challenges addressed as part of the government's review of primary care initiated in 1995.

The review took the form of a 'listening exercise' led by Gerald Malone, the Minister for Health. This resulted in a consultation paper published in June 1996 (Dorrell, 1996) followed by two white papers later in the year (Secretary of State for Health, 1996b and c). The consultation paper identified a number of key principles of good primary care. These were quality, fairness, accessibility, responsiveness and efficiency. It went on to summarise the issues that had arisen during the listening exercise in relation to each of the primary care services. On this basis an emerging agenda was suggested containing seven key themes:

1 *resources*: achieving a more equitable distribution, greater flexibility locally and an appropriate balance between primary and secondary care within the available resources;

2 *partnerships in care*: developing team and collaborative working between professionals, between primary and secondary care and with authorities and other agencies and also increasing the role of non-medical staff in providing care;

3 *developing professional knowledge*: through basic, post graduate and continuing education and training, research and clinical audit and with greater emphasis on multi-disciplinary approaches;

4 *patient and carer information and involvement*: developing choice and information but also recognizing patient responsibilities as well as rights;

5 *securing the workforce and premises (the basic building blocks of care)*: through action on GP recruitment; different approaches to contracts for GPs, pharmacists and optometrists to reflect changing workforce needs and to develop a multi-disciplinary approach; a more coherent approach to the primary care workforce and improving the standard and capacity of premises;

6 *better organization*: through linking practices together locally; better managerial support and organization; reducing bureaucracy and developing the IT infrastructure and the opportunities it affords;

7 *local flexibility*: by enabling different approaches to be taken to meet different local needs and circumstances.

These themes were then tested in an 'agenda setting round', again led by the Minister for Health, following which the first white paper was published in October 1996. This concentrated on the theme of flexibility, particularly for GPs, but also encompassing dentists, pharmacists and optometrists. In the case of GPs, the white paper proposed that GPs who wished should be able to choose a salaried option, either within partnerships or with other bodies, such as NHS trusts. It also put forward the idea of practice based contracts to enable primary care teams to take on additional responsibility for service provision. The theme of flexibility was underscored by proposals to use resources in support of these developments by removing the strict division between funds for general medical services and those for hospital and community health services.

The white paper emphasized that participation in the new arrangements would be voluntary. New forms of contract would be tested through a series of pilots which would be evaluated before being opened up more widely. Proposals for pilots were expected to emerge from within the NHS rather than being imposed by the centre. Legislation was published in the wake of the white paper to give legal force to these proposals with the aim of bringing them into operation in April 1998, subject to parliamentary approval.

The second white paper was published in December 1996. It focused on the remaining themes in the consultation document and made over 70 practical proposals for strengthening primary care. These included extending the nurse prescribing pilot scheme, improvements to GP vocational training, steps to provide more information to patients and carers about NHS services and how to use them appropriately, a more equitable distribution of funds for general medical services and community health services, and measures to improve premises. The white paper also made a series of recommendations concerned with the organization of primary care in recognition of the need to strengthen organizational and management capacity. These recommendations included the establishment of locality commissioning schemes to enable GPs in both fundholding and non-fundholding practices to manage resources at this level.

Taken together, the white papers and associated legislation served to put primary care at the heart of the NHS agenda. They were significant in part for the potentially far reaching nature of the changes proposed and in part for the way in which they were developed. The emphasis placed on listening to views from within the NHS, crystallizing these in a consultation document, testing the ensuing proposals through further consultation, and coming up with a programme of change to be implemented through formally evaluated pilot projects in advance of wide-spread implementation was in marked contrast to the way in which the NHS reforms were developed (*see* chapter 1). It was therefore not surprising that the primary care white papers were well received in most quarters, notwithstanding concerns that the strengths of British general practice might be undermined if the proposals were not implemented carefully.

The prospect that opened up was therefore of greater variety among primary care providers and even the emergence of a primary care market (Ham, 1996e). The choice of contractual options for GPs, the opportunity for new organizations like NHS trusts to become providers of primary care services, and the powers given to health authorities to use resources flexibly and to negotiate local contracts all pointed in this direction. In areas where standards of primary care were low, and where health authorities traditionally had few levers to bring about change, such as the inner cities, competition in primary care created new possibilities for improving quality, including using nurses and other staff to supplement the role of doctors. On the other hand, there were concerns that local contracting for primary care might increase transaction costs in the same way that had occurred in relation to hospital and community health services. There was also the risk that competition for contracts would make it more difficult to break down professional isolation between GPs and to build on the spirit of collaboration evident in the emergence of multifunds, total purchasing projects and co-operatives set up by family doctors to provide services to patients out of hours.

The implications for health authorities were equally profound. In particular, implementation of the changes set out in the white papers assumed a level of understanding about primary care that many authorities simply did not possess. Given the experience of most managers in running hospital and community health services this was to be expected, but it suggested the need for rapid progress up the learning curve to turn the proposals into action. The primary care agenda set out by the government also pointed to the need for health authorities to be able to specify standards for the provision of primary care and to develop arrangements for applying these standards to both new and established providers in order to provide adequate safeguards for patients. Indeed, with retail pharmacists indicating an interest in entering the primary care market and offering services in competition with GP partnerships, these issues assumed a degree of urgency.

Looking beyond the immediate proposals set out by the government, and taking into account developments within the NHS, it is possible to envisage a future in which primary care teams assume even greater responsibility for patient care. Initiatives in areas as diverse as Bromsgrove, Lyme Regis and Melton Mowbray suggest that GPs are actively integrating their services with those of the community health services, in some cases involving close links also with community hospitals. The emergence of 'primary managed care organizations', as they have been termed (Robinson, 1996), foreshadowed the development of British-style health maintenance organizations providing a one stop shop for patients in times of need (Smith *et al.*, 1997). These organizations operated on the philosophy that they should do what could be done appropriately in primary care and procure what could not be done from others. Typically they involved collaboration between GPs in different practices and functioned on a scale that demanded a more significant investment in management skills than has been usual in general practice. The development of alliances between GPs and NHS trusts providing community services in some areas indicated an alternative route to a similar destination.

Other parts of primary care were also affected by the government's proposals. In the case of dentistry, for example, the government announced plans to introduce on a pilot basis a system of local contracting. Beginning in 1998, health authorities will be able to negotiate with dentists for the provision of services to the community. As in the case of general medical services, the pilots will be evaluated and the government hopes that in this way some of the shortcomings of the general dental service can be overcome. One of the options likely to arise is the co-location of dental services with primary care teams as part of the further integration of services.

Labour's Plans

The shift away from competition as the main strategy of reform and the emphasis placed instead on primary care, clinical effectiveness, public health and *The Patient's Charter* had another important effect. Over time it resulted in a narrowing of the differences between the government and the Labour Party, a movement that was in turn influenced by changes in Labour's own position on the NHS. This movement was in part a pragmatic response to the difficulty of reversing the reforms, and in part it reflected the influence of the new leadership of the Labour Party. Instead of proposing to turn the clock back to the pre-reformed NHS, new Labour adopted a discriminating response to the reforms in which some elements were accepted, others were to be modified and yet others reversed. To be sure, important differences of philosophy and approach remained, but compared with the period around the genesis of the reforms, these differences appeared less important than the similarities.

The first major restatement of Labour's policy was published in June 1995 in a document entitled *Renewing the NHS* (Labour Party, 1995). This expressed strong opposition to the NHS market and to the move to commercialize health care and privatize elements of service provision. On the other hand, *Renewing the NHS* accepted the value of a separation of purchaser and provider responsibilities within the NHS, although it described this as a separation in the planning and delivery of health care. Under Labour's plans, the separation between planning and delivery was to be used not to promote competition but rather to ensure that providers were held accountable for the use of resources within a framework of cooperation and collaboration. Accountability would be achieved through the use of comprehensive health care agreements in place of annual contracts. These agreements would extend over a period of more than a year, in this way reducing transaction costs. *Renewing the NHS* went on to set out a promise to abolish GP fundholding on the grounds of its expense and the inequity it caused and to replace it with a system of GP commissioning in which health authorities would work together with GPs, through localities and GP commissioning groups, to determine which services to purchase.

In relation to the policy agenda, Labour placed particular emphasis on public health issues, including the need to prevent illness and tackle health inequalities. This was to be achieved by appointing a senior minister with responsibility for public health in government and by encouraging inter-departmental and inter-agency working on the causes of ill health. A promise was also made to set new targets for improving health going beyond those in the *Health of the Nation*. Other policy priorities included a new *Patient's Charter*, the development of a strategy to improve the quality of service provision, the further encouragement of community care, an emphasis on evidence based medicine and clinical effectiveness, and the development of primary care. Subsequent statements elaborating the commitments included in *Renewing the NHS* highlighted also the importance of reducing waiting times for treatment. This included a pledge to use the savings released by cutting back on management costs for this purpose.

On the key issue of NHS funding, Labour adopted a much more cautious approach than at the 1992 general election when specific commitments were made to increase the resources available within the NHS. This reflected Labour's concern to appear fiscally responsible and to avoid making promises on public expenditure which might be interpreted as necessitating tax increases. It also reflected a belief that existing resources could be used more wisely by reducing unnecessary bureaucracy and by increasing efficiency. This was reiterated by Tony Blair in a speech to the 1996 conference of the National Association of

Health Authorities and Trusts:

> 'As with any government, we can only spend, of course, what we can afford and it is not right or possible for any opposition party in this or any other area to write detailed spending plans whilst in opposition. But we understand and share the concerns about resource difficulties. But we must also see first, whether existing budgets are well spent – and the unnecessary form filling is removed. Second, that existing treatments are based on the best evidence and money is not being wasted on ineffective treatment. Only after these two stages have been gone through would a Labour government look at whether there was still a funding gap that needed to be bridged.'

The ideas contained in *Renewing the NHS* were taken a stage further in December 1996 in a speech by Labour's Shadow Health Secretary, Chris Smith. The speech outlined eight guiding objectives behind Labour's policy. These were:

1 resources should be allocated equitably so that health care is available on the basis of need;

2 there was a need to improve the quality of care at all levels in the NHS;

3 the cost of administration and management had to be cut to the minimum necessary to meet the NHS's fundamental aims;

4 NHS-funded services should continue to be provided by the NHS;

5 there was a need for a clearer national framework for service priorities;

6 there was value in separating health commissioning from responsibility for delivering health care;

7 it was essential to have a system that gave all GPs and other primary health care professionals a voice in shaping health services;

8 greater accountability and transparency was needed for the planning and funding decisions made by health authorities, hospitals and GPs.

Particular emphasis was placed on replacing fundholding with local commissioning groups of GPs covering populations of between 50,000 and 150,000 people. Under Labour's plans, GP commissioning groups would control resources for their patients, leaving health authorities free to concentrate on strategic commissioning. And while fundholding would be replaced over time with commissioning groups, it would still be possible for individual practices to hold a budget by agreement with other members of the group. This was variously interpreted as the Labour Party accepting fundholding and sounding its death knell, suggesting a degree of ambiguity in the extent to which Labour really was prepared to accept the reforms initiated by the government in this key area.

In one important respect, Smith's speech went beyond the policy set out in *Renewing the NHS*. This was in accepting a role for contestability as a force for improving standards. In other words, Labour explicitly acknowledged that cooperation and collaboration between those commissioning care and those providing services might not be sufficient to ensure high quality of care for patients. To give commissioning groups real leverage, they would be able to demand improvements in quality where standards were not acceptable and ultimately to move services to alternative providers if this failed to produce the desired change. Yet in arguing for contestability, Smith emphasized that this was quite different from the NHS market set up by the government. In essence, he maintained that Labour rejected both:

> 'a top-down system that is run and decided by consultants and executives'

and

> 'a market system based on hundreds of thousands of individual transactions all happening in uncoordinated and frequently contradictory fashion.'

Labour's policy represented:

'a third and better alternative: a devolved system, where decisions are taken close to the patient, but within a broader strategic structure that promotes equity and efficiency' (Smith, 1996).

These words unconsciously echoed those of Virginia Bottomley in her speech at the Royal Society of Medicine eighteen months earlier (*see* above) and illustrated the movement on the part of both major parties into the middle ground of the health policy debate. Coming as they did shortly after the publication of the white paper on the future of the NHS, restating the government's continuing commitment to the founding principles of the NHS and a health service funded through taxation, they demonstrated the convergence in thinking across the political spectrum on health service issues.

The main exception to convergence concerned the private finance initiative (PFI). This was launched in 1992 as a way of attracting private finance to pay for public sector capital projects. Initially, the PFI was of marginal importance in the NHS, being confined mainly to small schemes such as car parks and incinerators. However, under a change of rules published in 1995, NHS trusts wishing to undertake major capital schemes were required to seek private finance before they could be considered for Treasury support. The rules also enabled private finance to pay not only for the capital costs of NHS schemes but also for associated services such as catering, cleaning and in some cases clinical services (Ham, 1995).

This marked the beginning of a new phase of the PFI as applied to the NHS and it led to a number of large projects coming forward for funding in this way, including major hospital redevelopments. In practice negotiation over these projects proceeded slowly with both construction companies and financial institutions being critical of the government because of the complexity of the procedures involved and the degree of risk they were expected to take on. Also, as the House of Commons Treasury Committee pointed out, the PFI was being used as a substitute for public funding rather than a supplement. This was certainly the case in the NHS where the capital spending programme was cut significantly in anticipation of PFI projects coming to fruition.

Opponents of PFI argued that its use within the NHS would lead to privatisation through the back door. Not least, the change in the rules allowing private companies to run NHS services as well as construct new buildings under the terms of PFI suggested that the NHS was becoming a national health insurer, responsible for providing the funds to pay for health care but relying on an increasingly mixed economy of providers to deliver this care. Such a development had been hinted at by Virginia Bottomley who, in a newspaper article published in 1994, noted:

'We start by recognising that we have, in effect, redefined what we mean by the National Health Service. The service should not be defined by who provides it, but by the fundamental principle which underpins their work: to provide care on the basis of clinical need and regardless of the ability to pay . . . The precise nature of the services provided should increasingly become a matter for local decision. We should be open-minded about this . . . In the NHS of the future we can expect to see a much greater diversity of provision. The independent sector will supply some services, including direct patient care, under contract to health authorities and fundholders' (Bottomley, 1994).

It was this that Chris Smith was referring to in arguing that under Labour NHS funded services would continue to be provided by the NHS. As he stated:

'Unlike the Tories, we will not accept a redefining of the NHS to mean merely a socialised health insurance system, with backdoor privatisation of the running of services via either the Tories' version of the private finance initiative or the mechanisms of the Primary Care Bill that enable private companies to employ GPs . . . we have been clear that the NHS will not be privatised' (Smith, 1996).

Yet while there seemed to be clear water between the parties on this issue, the reality was more complex. Labour's Treasury team was in fact supportive of the principles of PFI while recognizing that health care was a more sensitive and difficult area for its application than transport and energy. The compromise that appeared to have been reached within the Labour Party was to accept the value of what were referred to as 'public/private partnerships', particularly in relation to the construction of new NHS facilities, but to insist that these did not extend into the running of services within these facilities. With the government also maintaining that clinical services should not be included in PFI projects, the differences between the parties on this issue became narrower than had seemed likely.

The International Context

While the United Kingdom has been at the forefront of recent efforts to reform the financing and delivery of health care, its experience is by no means unique. All around the world policy makers have been searching for new ways of increasing efficiency and ensuring that providers are responsive to service users. This reflects dissatisfaction with the effectiveness of existing policies and an interest in exploring alternative approaches. While the strategies pursued varied between countries, there were nevertheless a number of common themes (Ham, Robinson and Benzeval, 1990; OECD, 1992; Ham, 1997).

First, there was concern to strengthen the management of health services in order to reduce variations in performance and to introduce a stronger customer orientation. The 1983 *Griffiths Report* on general management exemplified this approach and its ideas were echoed elsewhere. By drawing on ideas from successful businesses, health policy makers sought to improve information systems, involve doctors, nurses and other staff in management, and devolve responsibility for management to hospitals and to units within hospitals. As an example, in Denmark hospitals in Copenhagen were run on an arm's length basis from the county council, while in parts of Italy steps were taken to strengthen hospital management, including running hospitals on a self governing basis. In some countries there was a move too to examine how services that were previously provided in the public sector could be supplied by private companies under contract to the public sector. The policy of strengthening management also involved the appointment of managers from inside and outside the health services to run hospitals and other facilities in a more professional fashion. Many of these initiatives were designed to manage clinical activity more effectively both by encouraging clinicians to play a bigger part in management and by motivating managers to question clinical practices more actively than had been the case in the past.

Second, there was an interest in making use of budgetary incentives as a way of improving performance. A key factor here was recognition that global budgets for hospitals and caps on doctors' fees were largely successful in containing overall levels of expenditure, but offered little or no incentive to those running hospitals to increase efficiency at the micro level. Policy makers therefore explored ways of combining cost control with payment systems that rewarded desired improvements in performance. This included altering the fee schedule for doctors, making use of capitation payments and experimenting with the use of cost per case payments for hospitals, such as diagnosis related groups. This was a key feature of the reforms introduced in some Swedish county councils, although experience suggested that it was difficult to reconcile the incentives of cost per case payments with overall budgetary control. Another kind of budgetary incentive was the use of patient charges or co-payments to moderate demand.

Third, there was a move in some countries to introduce market-like mechanisms into the health services (Saltman and von Otter, 1995). In no case did this involve abandoning planning in the pursuit of free market solutions. Rather, it meant searching for the middle ground in the belief that this would provide a more effective way of improving performance than established approaches. Thus, just as market oriented systems such as the United States showed greater interest in managed care, so systems that had traditionally relied on planning and regulation, like the Netherlands, New Zealand, Sweden and the United Kingdom, began testing out competitive strategies (*see* Figure 12). To this extent there was convergence around managed competition as a strategy of reform, although it should be emphasized that managed competition meant different things in different systems (Ham and Brommels, 1994). It should also be noted that enthusiasm for markets and competition waned not only in the United Kingdom (*see* above) but also in a number of other countries. In this respect, the process of reform came to resemble a pendulum with movement in one direction often being followed by an adjustment back in the opposite direction.

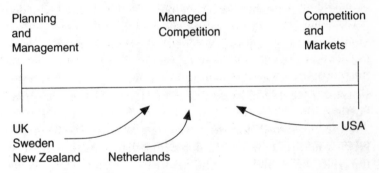

Figure 12: Trends in health care reforms.

As in the United Kingdom, disillusion with competition has been associated with a further phase of reform in which policy makers have launched a series of initiatives even in advance of conclusive evidence about the impact of earlier policies (Ham, 1997). For example, there was a concern to balance the focus on health services efficiency and responsiveness with greater attention to the influences on health which occur outside the health sector. Linked to this, there has been renewed interest in primary care and alternatives to hospital based medicine. And in line with a more questioning attitude to the benefits of health care technology, an increasing investment has been made in technology assessment and evidence based medicine. This in turn has been stimulated by discussion of the scope of publicly financed health care and whether the commitment to provide universal and comprehensive health services that has characterized policy development in OECD countries can be sustained in a climate of tax resistance and a reluctance to increase public spending.

As this discussion gathered pace, the key challenge facing policy makers became that of health care rationing or priority setting. With demands increasing as a result of the ageing population, advances in health care technology, and ever rising public expectations, and with the supply of resources constrained by both political and macro-economic considerations, steps were taken in a number of countries to examine priority setting more explicitly and systematically (*see* Box 11). The United Kingdom government chose not to follow the example of these countries, arguing that its role was to set the broad framework of priorities for the NHS at a national level, and that health authorities and GP fundholders were in the best position to interpret this framework at a local level in deciding on the use of their resources. Furthermore, in its white paper on the future of the NHS the government argued that there was no reason to believe that the NHS would become unaffordable and that annual increases in the NHS budget and a continuing drive to improve clinical effectiveness would be sufficient to deal with future pressures. In view of the importance of these issues, we discuss the challenge of priority setting in the NHS in the final part of this chapter.

Priority Setting

Rationing or priority setting in health care is not new but it is becoming more difficult (*see* Box 12). During the course of 1996, there were reports of NHS trusts not balancing their books, and accounts of health authorities having to consider desperate measures to cope with future funding pressures. Early in the 1996/97 financial year, the Department of Health allocated an

Box 11: Rationing in the NHS.

Rationing or priority setting has always been necessary in the NHS. In the past rationing occurred mainly through waiting lists. One of the effects of the NHS reforms has been to bring rationing out into the open. Examples of rationing decisions which have recently come to public attention include:

- the provision of long term and continuing care to elderly people and the disabled, which increasingly is becoming a responsibility of local authorities or of the individuals needing care and their families;

- the provision of intensive care for people who are critically ill where the number of beds available is not always sufficient to meet demand;

- the provision of new or emerging services like infertility treatment which are funded in different ways in different parts of the NHS;

- the funding of new drugs, such as beta interferon for the treatment of multiple sclerosis, which involve high costs and where the extent of the benefits is the subject of debate;

- the availability on the NHS of services such as tattoo removal, reversal of sterilization, gender reassignment and extraction of wisdom teeth which some people have argued should be left to personal responsibility;

- the priority to be attached to patients whose illnesses may in part be self inflicted, for example cigarette smokers waiting for heart surgery, when the demand for treatment exceeds supply.

additional £25 million to health authorities in England facing particularly severe difficulties, and further resources were provided later in the year in acknowledgement that the demands that existed within the NHS required extra funding. At the same time, the government agreed to increase the NHS budget for 1997/98 beyond the plans already announced. Notwithstanding these developments, there was a strong sense of deja vu, and a feeling that the wheel had turned full circle with the financial pressures that had forced Mrs Thatcher to set up her review of the NHS resurfacing. This led into a debate about health care rationing with a number of organizations calling on the government to address the challenge of choices in health care more directly (Royal College of Physicians, 1995; Rationing Agenda Group, 1996).

Yet before accepting that rationing is inevitable, it is important to acknowledge that existing budgets may be used inefficiently. This argument is often advanced by health economists and public health specialists who maintain that many medical interventions are unproven in their effectiveness (Maynard, 1996; Roberts *et al.*, 1996). They go on to suggest that even effective interventions may be provided inappropriately in some cases. Furthermore, variations in clinical practice patterns are invoked to demonstrate the opportunities that exist for achieving more health gain for the population without increasing health service funding, for example by making use of day surgery in place of inpatient stays where appropriate. Politicians have seized on these views to themselves argue that there is a need to improve clinical effectiveness within the NHS. A wide range of initiatives have been taken in support of this policy (*see* Box 12) and to encourage the more widespread adoption of evidence based medicine.

Box 12: Policy initiatives on clinical effectiveness.

A wide range of initiatives have been taken to improve clinical effectiveness and to make medicine evidence based. These include:

- the NHS Centre for Reviews and Dissemination at the University of York which disseminates the results of health care research in the NHS;

- the UK Cochrane Centre which maintains a database of systematically reviewed randomized controlled trials of relevance to health care and disseminates the results to the NHS;

- the Central Health Outcomes Unit which aims to encourage and co-ordinate the development and use of information on health outcomes;

- the UK Clearing House for Information on the Assessment of Health Outcomes which acts as a central reference point for work on outcome measurement.

Much of the work in this field is supported through the research and development programme. The programme also includes expenditure on technology assessment in health care aimed at evaluating the effectiveness of new methods of diagnosis and treatment. Important publications include the *Effective Health Care Bulletins,* the *Register of Cost Effectiveness Studies,* and national guidance in the form of *EL(93)115* and *EL(94)74.*

While this policy has attracted widespread support, to the extent that developments in the United Kingdom are perceived by some countries as an example to emulate, it remains an open question as to whether the emphasis on improving clinical effectiveness will ultimately increase or reduce expenditure. This is because evidence based medicine will almost certainly result in the increased use of interventions of proven effectiveness as well as the reduced use of interventions of questionable effectiveness. What is more, experience in the NHS indicates how difficult it is to release resources through strategies designed to improve clinical effectiveness, suggesting that estimates that £1billion could be saved by acting on the evidence of effectiveness may be unreliable (Michael Peckham quoted in Timmins, 1996). These strategies are of course worth pursuing but mainly on the basis that they will improve the quality of care rather than that they will save money. Given the uncertainties involved in clinical decisions it will never be possible to use resources without incurring inefficiencies and there are therefore limits to what the 'new scientism' (Klein *et al.*, 1996) in health care can be expected to achieve.

To make this point is not to argue that there is therefore a need to take a more radical approach to priority setting, for example by excluding some services entirely from NHS coverage. Not only has this approach already been rejected by the government, which has argued against 'blanket exclusions' from the NHS, but also, as international experience shows (*see* Box 13), those countries that have tackled priority setting on a more explicit and systematic basis have on the whole chosen not to go down this route. Rather, it is to suggest that a strategic approach is needed encompassing the use of techniques to ensure that resources are used efficiently (including clinical guidelines and an investment in health technology assessment), further research into ways of changing clinical behaviour in line with evidence of effectiveness, and methods of involving the public and the health care professions in debating the choices that have to be made and influencing these choices. As the government has recognized, such an approach has to acknowledge the different levels at which priorities are set – nationally, locally and in relation to individual patients. It also needs to take into account the long timescale over which change is likely to occur.

Box 13: International approaches to priority setting.

The most famous attempt to set priorities in a more systematic way is that undertaken in the state of **Oregon**. This centres on the Medicaid programme of health care for people who are poor and on low incomes. To bring more people into the scope of Medicaid, Oregon appointed a Health Services Commission to rank services in order of priority. By restricting coverage to high priority services, it was possible to extend the reach of Medicaid. Priorities were set on the basis of values expressed by the public, evidence on the effectiveness of different services, and the judgement of Commission members. After a number of years of development, the Oregon list was eventually implemented in 1994 with 565 services out of 696 being funded.

The Core Services Committee set up by the **New Zealand** government in 1992 rejected the Oregon approach, arguing that setting priorities by drawing up a simple list of services to be funded was not appropriate. Instead it maintained that the services already funded should continue to be funded and it went on to make a broad assessment of priorities. In addition, the Committee organized a series of consensus conferences on particular treatments and services, and on this basis set out guidelines for the provision of these services. Work was also undertaken on the configuration of highly specialized services and on the development of clinical criteria to determine priority on waiting lists.

In the **Netherlands**, the report of the Dunning Committee, published in 1991, offered advice to the Dutch government on how priorities should be set in the reformed social insurance system. The report outlined a framework for thinking about priorities, involving the use of four criteria to judge whether a service should be funded. These criteria entailed asking whether care was necessary from the community's point of view, whether it was effective and efficient, and whether it could be left to individuals to pay for directly. The Dunning Committee's framework has been tested on a number of services and a programme of work has been undertaken on health technology assessment and on the development of clinical guidelines and protocols.

A number of Nordic countries have also approached priority setting in a more explicit fashion. **Norway** was the first to do so with the report of the Lonning Committee in 1987 followed by **Sweden** and **Finland**. In the Swedish case, a parliamentary priorities commission has set out an ethical platform for determining priorities based on three principles: human dignity, equity and efficiency. In this respect, the Swedish approach is similar to that of the Netherlands in suggesting a method for approaching priority setting rather than a detailed list.

In the absence of a strategic approach, the main responsibility for setting priorities within the NHS rests with clinicians in relation to individual patients and with health authorities and GP fundholders for local populations. Research evidence indicates that some health authorities have begun to discuss exclusions from their contracts, despite advice from the government to the contrary (Redmayne, 1995). In addition, health authorities have restricted the resources available for low priority services, such as infertility treatment, and have drawn up guidelines to determine who should receive access to these services. In some cases too use has been made of techniques drawn from health economics and epidemiology, and steps have been taken to consult with the public. Notwithstanding this work, most decisions remain strongly influenced by historical commitments and a great deal remains to be done to bridge the gap between research and practice.

The responsibility placed on health authorities and fundholders to set priorities may result in different decisions in different districts. This brings into question the principle of equity on which the NHS is based and raises the issue of whether a *national* health service still exists. The government has so far held to the line that its role is to set the national framework of priorities in the annual guidance issued to the NHS and in the white paper on the future of the NHS it explicitly rejected the argument that:

'the Government should prescribe at a national level what treatments the NHS should provide . . . No such list of treatments could ever hope to accommodate the range and complexity of the different cases which individual clinicians face all the time. There would be a real risk of taking decisions out of the hands of the clinicians treating patients and into the hands of others who possess neither the experience of caring for patients nor the expertise to make such decisions' (Secretary of State for Health, 1996a).

In practice this means that when difficult choices arise health authorities have to take responsibility for these choices, including explaining why funding for individual patients may not be available. This was well illustrated in 1995 by the case of Child B, a 10 year old girl with leukaemia whose family requested that the health authority concerned pay for a second bone marrow transplant. On the basis of clinical advice, the health authority declined to do so and when its decision was challenged in the courts it had to explain both to the judges and to the media why resources were not available for this purpose. The locus of responsibility for these decisions will remain at a local level for as long as the government maintains that it is not appropriate to go beyond the current framework of priorities at a national level. Indeed, in a situation in which the Labour Party also appears to have come down against a more systematic approach to priority setting along the lines pursued in other countries, muddling through seems set to continue. Consistent with Klein's observation on the management of the NHS, the stance taken by politicians illustrates that when things go well those at the centre take the credit, but when the going gets tough they prefer to devolve the blame (Klein, 1995b).

The bigger question raised by the rationing debate is whether the NHS really is affordable now and in the future and whether the commitment to a health service providing services from the cradle to the grave can be sustained. However decisions on priorities are made, and wherever responsibility for these decisions rests, it is this question that continues to be debated. On the one side of the argument is the view of groups like Healthcare 2000 (1995) and evidence from within the NHS itself about the gap between available resources and demands; on the other side of the argument is the position taken by the government and some independent analysts (Harrison *et al.*, 1997) which holds that the NHS is affordable despite the pressures which confront health authorities and trusts. It is this debate that seems set to continue and to dominate discussion of health policy for the foreseeable future.

Conclusion

To return to the starting point of this book, the clear implication is that notwithstanding the benefits that have resulted from the NHS reforms, the long term underfunding of the NHS continues to present a major challenge to policy makers. The additional resources made available by the government to assist the implementation of the reforms undoubtedly helped to ease the funding pressures in the early 1990s, enabling progress to be made in a number of areas of service development. The much lower levels of expenditure growth experienced in the mid 1990s, coupled with increasing demands, caused these pressures to return. This suggests that the NHS will be able to continue providing a universal and comprehensive service if governments allocate resources through the public expenditure system in line with the increases of the early 1990s. If this does not happen then supplementary forms of funding, including raising additional income from patient charges and co-payments, may become inevitable. This is ultimately a matter of social and political choice reflecting the values which shape decisions on taxation and spending and the future of welfare services including health care. The kind of health service that will be provided in the next millennium hinges on the outcome of this choice.

References

Appleby J (1994) *Developing Contracting*. National Association of Health Authorities and Trusts, Birmingham.

Appleby J (1995) *Testing the Market*. National Association of Health Authorities and Trusts, Birmingham.

Audit Commission (1995) *Briefing on GP Fundholding*. HMSO, London.

Audit Commission (1996) *What the Doctor Ordered*. HMSO, London.

Black D, Birchall A and Trimble I (1994) Non-fundholding in Nottingham: a vision of the future. *British Medical Journal*: 309; 930–2.

Bloor K and Maynard A (1993) *Expenditure on the NHS During and After the Thatcher Years*. Centre for Health Economics, University of York.

Bloor K and Maynard A (1994) An outsider's view of the NHS reforms. *British Medical Journal*: 309; 352–3.

Bottomley V (1994) National health, local dynamic. *The Independent*, 22 August.

Bottomley V (1995) *The NHS: continuity and change*. Department of Health, London.

Bradlow J and Coulter A (1993) Effect of fundholding and indicative prescribing scheme on general practitioners' prescribing costs. *British Medical Journal*: 307; 1186–9.

96f) Managed markets in health care: the UK experi-
lth Policy: 35; 279–92.

) (1997) *Health Care Reform: learning from interna-
rience*. Open University Press, Buckingham.

t al. (1989) *Managed Competition*. King's Fund
ondon.

obinson R and Benzeval M (1990) *Health Check*.
l Institute, London.

l Heginbotham C (1991) *Purchasing Together*. King's
ge, London.

d Haywood S (1992) *The NHS Guide*. National
of Health Authorities and Trusts, Birmingham.

chofield D and Williams J (1993) *Partners in
National Association of Health Authorities and
ingham.

l Brommels M (1994) Health care reform in the
, Sweden and the United Kingdom. *Health Affairs*:
-19.

et al. (1997) Can the NHS cope in future? *British
rnal*: **314**; 139–42.

2000 (1995) *UK Health and Healthcare Services:
d policy options*. Shire Hall, London.

nent Trends (1993) *Local bargaining in the NHS: a
t and second wave trusts*.

Brindle D (1993a) Dangerous time for a famous name. *The Guardian*, 28 July.

Brindle D (1993b) Casualties in a war of words. *The Guardian*, 20 October.

Butler J (1992) *Patients, Policies and Politics*. Open University Press, Buckingham.

Clinical Standards Advisory Group (1993) *Access to and Availability of Specialist Services*. HMSO, London.

Coulter A (1995) Evaluating general practice fundholding in the United Kingdom. *European Journal of Public Health*: 5; 233–39.

Department of Health (1993a) *Virginia Bottomley reaffirms commitment to the underlying principles of the NHS*. DoH, London (press release).

Department of Health (1993b) *Making London Better*. Health Publications Unit, Lancashire.

Department of Health (1993c) *Managing the New NHS*. DoH, London.

Dixon J and Glennerster H (1995) What do we know about fundholding in general practice? *British Medical Journal*: **311**; 727–30.

Dixon J and Harrison A (1997) Funding the NHS: a little local difficulty? *British Medical Journal*: **314**; 216–19.

Dorrell S (1996) *Primary Care: the future*. NHS Executive, London.

Enthoven AC (1985) *Reflections on the Management of the NHS*. Nuffield Provincial Hospitals Trust, London.

Fowler N (1991) *Ministers Decide*. Chapman, London.

Ghodse B (1995) Extracontractual referrals: safety valve or administrative paperchase? *British Medical Journal*: 310; 1573–6.

Glennerster H *et al.* (1992) *A Foothold for Fundholding*. King's Fund Institute, London.

Glennerster H *et al.* (1994) *Implementing GP Fundholding*. Open University Press, Buckingham.

Graffy J and Williams J (1994) Purchasing for all: an alternative to fundholding. *British Medical Journal*: 308; 391–4.

Ham C (1989) Clarke's strong medicine. *Marxism Today*: March, 38–41.

Ham C (1990a) *The New National Health Service: organization and management*. Radcliffe Medical Press, Oxford.

Ham C (1990b) *Holding On While Letting Go*. King's Fund College, London.

Ham C (1991) Revisiting the internal market. *British Medical Journal*: 302; 250–1.

Ham C (1992a) *Health Policy in Britain* (3rd edition). Macmillan, Basingstoke.

Ham C (1992b) *Locality Purchasing*. Health Services Management Centre, University of Birmingham.

Ham C (1992c) *Managed Competi prospects*. Manchester Statistical S

Ham C (1992d) Growing pain *Guardian*, 5 September.

Ham C (1993a) How go the N *Journal*: 306; 77–8.

Ham C (1993b) Reviewing the *Journal*: 307; 5–6.

Ham C (1993c) The latest reorg *Medical Journal*: 307; 1089–90.

Ham C (1994) Where now for the *Journal*: 309; 351–2.

Ham C (1995) Profiting from the 310; 415–16.

Ham C (1996a) Population-cer chasing. *The Milbank Quarterly*

Ham C (1996b) *Public, Private the NHS?* DEMOS, London.

Ham C (1996c) The future of th 313; 1277–8.

Ham C (1996d) Contestability: *British Medical Journal*: 312; 7(

Ham C (1996e) A primary care 313; 127–8.

Ham C (1 ment. *He

Ham C ((tional exp

Ham C Institute,

Ham C, King's Fu

Ham C a Fund Co

Ham C Associati

Ham C, *Purchasin* Trusts, B

Ham C Netherla **Winter;** 1

Harrison *Medical*

Healthca *challenge*

IRS Emp *survey of*

Jarman B (1994) *The Crisis in London Medicine: how many hospital beds does the capital need?* University of London, London.

Jones D, Lester C and West R (1994) *Monitoring changes in health services for older people.* In Robinson and Le Grand *op cit.*

Klein R *et al.* (1996) *Managing Scarcity.* Open University Press, Buckingham.

Klein R (1995a) Big bang health care reform – does it work?: The case of Britain's 1991 National Health Service reforms. *The Milbank Quarterly:* 73; 299–337.

Klein R (1995b) *The New Politics of the NHS* (3rd edition). Longmans, London.

Labour Party (1995) *Renewing the NHS.* Labour Party, London.

Laing W (1990) *Laing's Review of Private Health Care 1990/91.* Laing Buisson Publications, London.

Lawson N (1992) *The View from No. 11.* Bantam Press, London.

Le Grand J (1994) *Evaluating the NHS reforms.* In Robinson and Le Grand *op cit.*

Maxwell R (1994) *What Next for London's Health Care?* King's Fund, London.

Maynard A (1996) Table manners at the health care feast. *Eurohealth:* 2; 6–7.

Maynard A and Bloor K (1996) Introducing a market to the United Kingdom's national health service. *The New England Journal of Medicine:* 334; 604–8.

National Audit Office (1995) *Contracting for Acute Health Care in England.* HMSO, London.

NHSME (1989) *Role of District Health Authorities – analysis of issues.* London.

NHSME (1990) *Developing Districts.* London.

NHSME (1991) *Assessing Health Care Needs.* London.

NHSME (1992) *Local Voices.* London.

OECD (1992) *The Reform of Health Care: a comparative analysis of seven OECD countries.* OECD, Paris.

OECD (1994) *OECD Economic Surveys: United Kingdom 1994.* OECD, Paris.

Petchey R (1995) General practitioner fundholding: weighing the evidence. *The Lancet*: **346**; 1139–42.

Radical Statistics Health Group (1992) NHS reforms; the first six months – proof of progress or a statistical smokescreen? *British Medical Journal*: **304**; 705–9.

Radical Statistics Health Group (1995) NHS 'indicators of success': what do they tell us? *British Medical Journal*: **310**; 1045–50.

Raftery J *et al.* (1996) Contracting in the NHS quasi-market. *Health Economics*: **5**; 353–62.

Rationing Agenda Group (1996) *The Rationing Agenda in the NHS.* King's Fund, London.

Redmayne S (1995) *Reshaping the NHS*. National Association of Health Authorities and Trusts, Birmingham.

Roberts C *et al.* (1996) The wasted millions. *Health Service Journal*: **10 October**; 24–7.

Roberts J (1990) Kenneth Clarke: hatchet man or remoulder? *British Medical Journal*: **301**; 1383–6.

Robinson B (1996) *Primary managed care: the Lyme alternative.* In Meads G (ed) *Future Options for General Practice*. Radcliffe Medical Press, Oxford.

Robinson R and Le Grand J (eds) (1994) *Evaluating the NHS Reforms*. King's Fund Institute, London.

Royal College of Physicians (1995) *Setting Priorities in the NHS.* London.

Saltman R and von Otter C (eds) (1995) *Implementing Planned Markets in Health Care*. Open University Press, Buckingham.

Secretary of State for Health and others (1989) *Working for Patients*. HMSO, London.

Secretary of State for Health (1996a) *The National Health Service: a service with ambitions*. HMSO, London.

Secretary of State for Health (1996b) *Choice and Opportunity*. The Stationery Office, London.

Secretary of State for Health (1996c) *Primary Care: delivering the future*. The Stationery Office, London.

Smith C (1996) *A health service for a new century*. Text of speech delivered on 3 December 1996.

Smith J *et al.* (1997) *Beyond Fundholding*. Health Services Management Centre, University of Birmingham and Centre for Health Planning and Management, University of Keele.

Smith R (1991) William Waldegrave: thinking beyond the new NHS. *British Medical Journal*: 302; 711–14.

Timmins N (1995) *The Five Giants*. HarperCollins, London.

Timmins N (1996) NHS 'wastes £1bn on ineffective treatments'. *The Independent*, 2 January.

Tomlinson Report (1992) *Report of the Inquiry into London's Health Services, Medical Education and Research*. HMSO, London.

Further Reading

This book is meant to provide an introduction to the reformed NHS rather than a comprehensive assessment. Readers seeking further information may do so by following up the articles and books listed in the references. In addition, the following sources are recommended. John Butler's book, *Patients, Policies and Politics*, offers a clear overview of the review which led up to the reforms, the debate which followed their announcement, and the early stages of implementation (Butler, 1992). The collection of papers edited by Ray Robinson and Julian Le Grand (1994) is the most comprehensive early assessment of the reforms as a whole. Rudolf Klein's book, *The New Politics of the NHS*, offers a lucid analytical history of the NHS, with chapter 6 focusing particularly on the reforms (Klein, 1995b). The Audit Commission's study of fundholding includes a useful evaluation of one of the most controversial aspects of the reforms (Audit Commission, 1996). The author's own assessment (Ham, 1996f) brings together data from a number of sources in an attempt to draw up a balance sheet.

Index